The Care
& Preservation of
TEXTILES

To all those
who helped create
The Textile Conservation Centre,
Hampton Court Palace

The Care
& Preservation of
TEXTILES

KAREN FINCH, o.b.e.
& GRETA PUTNAM

Foreword by Donald King
former Keeper of the Department of Textiles and Dress
Victoria & Albert Museum, London

B.T. BATSFORD LTD, London

First published 1985
© Karen Finch and Greta Putnam 1985

Based on *Caring for Textiles*, by Karen
Finch and Greta Putnam, published by
Barrie & Jenkins, 1977

ISBN 0 7134 4411 8

Typeset by Servis Filmsetting Ltd, Manchester
and printed in Great Britain by
Anchor Brendon Ltd, Tiptree, Essex
for the publishers
B.T. Batsford Ltd
4 Fitzhardinge Street
London W1H 0AH

Contents

150203

Acknowledgements

We would like to acknowledge the help and advice we have received from our colleagues and friends in all our endeavours, with our special gratitude to Miss Anne Buck, O.B.E. and Mrs Stella M. Newton, O.B.E.

We also thank the following individuals and institutions for granting us permission to reproduce photographs of objects in their possession not already acknowledged in the text: Her Majesty the Queen; Michael Adda; All Saints Church, Culmstock; Mrs D. Briscoe; Barleston Church, Stoke-on-Trent; Colchester Museum; Derbyshire Museum Service; The Irish Georgian Society; Anthony and Victoria Jarvis; Lennox Money; Levens Heritage; D. McAlpine; Barbara Mullins; The National Trust; J. Partington; Mrs Sluman; The Victoria & Albert Museum; The Wallace Collection.

We are grateful to Danielle Bosworth for allowing us to reproduce the line drawings which illustrated *Caring for Textiles* and for photographs by the following: John and Pegaret Anthony, Antony Bock, Barry Castelete, Laurie Connon, Stephen Cousens, Graham Frear, Quill Publishing, Chris Steele-Perkins, Victoria & Albert Museum and the staff and students of the Textile Conservation Centre.

Foreword
BY DONALD KING

Textiles are made to be used and, eventually, they become worn out and are discarded. But they can also be things of great beauty, historical interest or sentimental value, and in these cases it is natural that we should try to preserve them. This is not easy for, even if we protect them from the friction and soiling of normal use and the strains of repeated cleaning, they remain under continuous attack from their environment – from light which fades the dyes and weakens the fibres, from changing temperature and humidity which makes the threads work and twist as they take up and give out moisture, and from dirt and chemicals in the air which tend to destroy the fabric. As the authors of this book say, 'considering everything, it is a wonder that textiles survive for any length of time at all'.

Nevertheless, many do survive, sometimes for centuries, and there is a growing feeling that we should try to do more to ensure the preservation of fine old textiles. This feeling arises from a number of factors. The opening of the great country houses to the public has revealed the existence of many beautiful old textiles, some of which are in an advanced state of decrepitude. The increasing interest in collecting antiques of every sort has extended to the field of textiles and many of these, too, stand in need of conservation treatment. Also, many people who live surrounded by the myriad mechanically-produced artifacts of the modern world have developed an understanding and respect for the beauties of hand-craftsmanship, and wish to employ their own handicraft skills to preserve old examples for future generations.

The present book on *The Care and Preservation of Textiles*, an enlarged and revised version of an earlier work by the same authors, will be an invaluable aid to all who are interested in this field. One of its authors, Karen Finch, trained in the Danish textile tradition, subsequently brought her skills to England and did remarkable conservation work on the textile collections of the Victoria & Albert Museum. Later she set up her own workshop and, in 1975, became the first Principal of the admirable Textile Conservation Centre at Hampton Court Palace. Both her fellow-author, Greta Putnam, and the illustrator, Danielle Bosworth, have been her trusted associates for many years. They are all experts in textile conservation and their book incorporates their long experience and profound knowledge of the field. It is not, however, a manual for professional conservationists, but a practical guide for all those who own or are otherwise responsible for the care of historic textiles. It examines all the questions which most frequently arise and provides straightforward answers in plain language. It lays down basic principles for protective housekeeping and gives detailed instructions for the treatment of the various categories of furnishing textiles, costume and so on. It describes clearly how to clean, repair and mount the various kinds of textiles. And it is particularly good in drawing the very important dividing line between, on the one hand, the kinds of cleaning and repair which can properly be undertaken by anyone with reasonable skills in washing and needlework and, on the other hand, the cases in which it is imperative to consult a professional conservationist.

I know, from the innumerable questions on this subject which have been addressed to me in the past, that this book is much needed. I shall certainly recommend it to future questioners, and I am confident that all who read it will find in it precisely the kind of advice that they require. It is a thoroughly practical guide and one which should do much to raise standards of care in the field of antique textiles.

Donald King
Former Keeper of the Department of Textiles
and Dress
Victoria & Albert Museum, London

Introduction

Our earlier book, *Caring for Textiles*, was written in answer to the many questions asked by those who owned or had charge of textiles and, aware of the importance of their preservation, wished to know how to care for them.

This present book contains much of the information contained in the previous book, brought up-to-date and amended where necessary.

We still strongly advise owners or custodians of textiles to consult an acknowledged textile historian before making any arrangements regarding treatment and, if advised that the piece is of cultural importance, worthy of the greatest care to preserve the evidence it may hold, to seek the advice of a trained and qualified textile conservator regarding the treatment proper to its importance.

When we gave this advice earlier, trained textile conservators were not numerous nor was it easy to get work done quickly, as those already trained and working were trying to reduce the backlog of conservation work which had accumulated as the need for their expertise had been acknowledged.

Now, however, more conservators have finished training courses and the waiting time for work to be done is greatly reduced. In the case of extremely large textiles, such as tapestries, however, the job can take a long time.

We aim to give readers an understanding of why textiles deteriorate and what can be done in the way of preventive conservation – the first and safest line of defence against all the causes and some of the effects of deterioration.

Some readers may be collectors of textiles or other objects with textile connections. The care of such collections may require specialist knowledge beyond this, more general, book. Other readers may be interested in the textile arts from the point of creating new work. We hope that the section devoted to various specialist societies and teaching institutions may encourage application for information or membership and that the bibliography recommends some books which will prove interesting and helpful.

We have given examples of some conservation/restoration treatments so that those who contemplate such work on their own textiles will have some idea of what this involves, and thus be in a more informed position to decide whether to go ahead or to seek the opinion of a trained conservator. In the case of a collection of textiles on display in a historic house, professional advice should always be sought both from a textile historian and a qualified conservator.

There are new chapters in this book on volunteers and the valuable work they can do, and on the importance of colour, especially in relation to enhancing the effective display of textiles.

Textiles and fibres:
A general survey

Think of your forefathers, think of your posterity!
John Quincy Adam

The term 'textile' is used to cover a very wide range of objects. A large woven tapestry hanging on the wall of a historic house is a textile, but so is a piece of delicate lace. Clothes and many clothing accessories, household linen, soft furnishings such as curtains and upholstery fabrics, embroideries, carpets and rugs, flags and banners, church vestments, altar frontals and other church furnishings are all textiles, as also are parts of dolls, parasols and fans and countless other objects.

A history of textiles is virtually a history of civilisation, for man, all over the world, has made textiles from earliest times: nets to catch food and fabrics to cover himself for warmth, decoration and visual enjoyment. It is not known exactly when man began to weave but there are cave pictures from about 5000 B.C. which show primitive looms. Greek and Roman writers have described, with admiration, Babylonian tapestries which, they said, depicted rich garments, heavily embroidered and interwoven with gold. This would have required weaving of a sophisticated kind. Although these Babylonian tapestries have not themselves survived there are wall-paintings and decorations on pottery which show that even everyday clothes of the time were decorated with patterns in different colours. Balls of coloured wools, dating back to 2000 B.C., were found around the turn of this century by Sir Flinders Petrie in Egyptian tombs, and burial clothes have been found by other archaeologists in graves as far apart as Scandinavia and Peru.

1 *Flower faces woven into decoration of a child's tunic. An example of early tapestry weaving.*

Very few ancient textiles have survived and those which have were, for the most part, found in tombs. The Egyptian tombs in particular were very favourable for the safe-keeping of textiles, being cool and dark with an even temperature and humidity and having unpolluted air. Apart from the occasional grave robber, the textiles would have been undisturbed for centuries. Some of the burial garments unearthed from tombs disintegrated on exposure to outside conditions, but others have survived to find their way into museums and collections.

During the middle ages, textiles, particularly tapestries and bed hangings, were of such importance that they were always put at the head of the list of valuables in wills and inventories. Many of the earliest textiles which have survived in this country are tapestries, which have always been costly and therefore treasured, and ecclesiastical embroideries, which again were valuable because of the materials used, including gold and silver. The latter survived also because of the care they received from church or religious orders to which they belonged.

From the twelfth to the fifteenth centuries England was famous all over Europe for embroidery of remarkable beauty. Known as Opus Anglicanum – English work – this embroidery used materials of great value, particularly gold and silver thread, and the design and workmanship was of the highest quality. The output of the workrooms, staffed by professional (for the most part male) embroiderers who had served a seven-year apprenticeship, was sold by merchants who made this their special trade. Most of the embroideries were of religious subjects and were sold to churches for the decoration of vestments. Opus Anglicanum is mentioned no less than 113 times in a Vatican inventory of 1295. Embroidery was also done by nuns and there is a record, dated 1271, of an altar frontal for Westminster Abbey which had taken four women four years to complete. Quite a number of examples of Opus Anglicanum have survived and can be seen in museums, with perhaps the best known being the famous Syon Cope at the

2 *Detail of Opus Anglicanum embroidery of the fifteenth century from a church in Devon.*

Victoria & Albert Museum in London.

For many generations English gentlewomen were taught to embroider as part of their education. Some stately houses employed professional designers and embroidresses, and ladies at court and in castles throughout the land spent many hours at their needlework.

In other ways, too, the history of Britain is closely connected with textiles, and those which have survived to the present day are part of our heritage and need our care and protection if they are to give pleasure and knowledge of the past to those who come after us.

Fibres

All textiles are made from fibres, which can be animal, vegetable or man-made. These fibres might be matted together to form a material in the way that wool can be matted to form felt, or they might be pulped with water and then beaten out, as the Indonesians still do with the tree-bark fibres from which they made bark cloth. More familiarly, fibres can be spun into yarn and the yarn can be fashioned into lace, knitted or crocheted, made into net, or knotted into trimmings and decorations as in tatting or macramé. But, most common of all, fibres can be spun into yarn and woven on a loom to make a fabric.

The properties and characteristics of the fibres from which a textile is made will always play some part in its reaction to the treatment it receives and the environment in which it is kept. Textiles made earlier than the middle of the nineteenth century were almost certainly constructed from natural fibres. These fibres are not, of course, designed by nature to be made into fabrics but have their own natural functions; because of that, they will always retain some of the characteristics required to fulfil those functions, even though man has taken the fibres and used them for his own purposes by treating them, spinning and dyeing them and weaving them into material.

Wool

Wool is, by nature, intended to keep the animal on which it grows warm and dry, and it will, even when spun and woven into a material, still retain the ability to absorb up to one-third of its own weight in water without feeling damp to the touch. Indeed, wool needs an atmosphere in which there is a certain degree of moisture if it is not to become hard, dry and brittle. In their natural state, wool fibres are elastic and spring back after being stretched. Woollen material, too, resists being pressed into sharp folds and tends to spring back again. For instance, permanent pleating of woollen material, like permanent waving of human hair, can only be achieved by irreversibly damaging the cell structure of the fibres of wool and hair.

Wool tends to decompose under the action of strong sunlight and reacts unfavourably to heat, but it will last and store well in favourable conditions. Apart from sunlight and dry heat, wool is liable to be attacked by insect pests such as moths and carpet beetles, and by mildew. Because of their cell structure, wool fibres shrink and mat together if washed and rubbed in hot soapy water. With care, however, wool will wash successfully.

Wool does not readily burn, but if it comes into contact with a naked flame its fibres decompose, giving off a smell similar to that of burning feathers. If the flame is removed, the wool does not continue to burn, but each fibre forms a black charred knob.

Silk

Silk is a natural thread which is spun by the silkworm, *Bombyx mori*, into a cocoon to protect itself whilst a pupa and from which it eventually emerges as a moth. Silk fibres are slightly less elastic than wool but, because they are so long, smooth and fine, they can be woven into a soft, luxurious material, which drapes and hangs in beautiful folds. In manufacture, the gum-like sericin which holds the silk threads together in the cocoon is removed from the natural silk and this loss may be replaced in various ways, sometimes with metallic salts, producing 'weighted' silk. This presents problems in the care of silk material, especially if the amount of weighting is considerable, as was often the case in black silk or silk used in the making of fringes or tassels. Weighted silk can seldom be washed successfully. Sunlight and hot, dry conditions cause all silk, but especially weighted silk, to become dry and brittle, although pure silk and good quality silk embroidery threads have longer lasting qualities. If silk comes into contact with a flame it will burn, giving off a singed smell similar to burning hair or horn.

Linen

Linen is made from fibres which originally held the stems of the flax plant upright, and carried moisture up through the plant to the leaves and flowers. Linen fibres, produced from the retted (water-softened) stems of the flax plant, even when woven into cloth, will always attract and carry moisture along themselves. Linen is always stronger when wet than when dry, washes well and can be dry-cleaned.

Cotton

Cotton fibres come from the seed heads or bolls of the cotton plant. Cotton has greater resistance to high temperatures than most other fibres and can be kept in storage for a long time without deterioration. Sunlight causes gradual loss of strength in cotton and yellowing of white cotton fabrics. Cotton fibres, like linen, are stronger when wet than when dry and, indeed, humidity is necessary when weaving cotton, as anyone who knows of the traditional cotton weaving industry in Lancashire will testify. Cotton burns very readily if brought into contact with a naked flame. It can be dyed successfully but dyeing other vegetable fibres, especially linen, has not always been easy. Cotton is fairly resistant to solvents and will generally dry-clean successfully.

Man-made fibres

Man-made fibres fall into two main groups, depending on the origin of the materials used to make them. There are those fibres made from materials with a natural origin, such as cellulose or protein; rayon is an example of a material made from fibres in this group. The other group consists of synthetic fibres; polyester materials and nylon are examples of this group.

Identification is not easy and man-made fibres are now so numerous and varied that it would be impossible to do more here than advise that one should determine the characteristics of each before choosing which one to use. Fortunately many, even bought from the roll, have

quite good descriptive labels regarding care and treatment. This information is essential. Some will dry clean successfully and others will not, most are washable, some are more flammable than others, some have the advantage of being stable and resistant to light but some are adversely affected by heat. Most of them are chemically inert and will generally combine quite successfully with natural fibres. Those man-made fibres which are known to have stable qualities and good resistance to light can be used in conservation as supporting materials. By being aware of the characteristics of fibres, care can be taken in choosing materials for new work and also in deciding on the most suitable methods of cleaning and conservation of old fabrics. The nature of the fibres used must always be considered in assessing how materials could react.

Deterioration of textiles

All textiles start to suffer from deterioration the moment they are made. There are many reasons for this apart from ordinary wear and tear to which, of course, very precious or special textiles would not be subjected to any great degree.

The greatest enemy of all textiles is light – not only visible light but also the ultra violet radiation in daylight and that emitted by fluorescent tube lighting. Light not only causes dyes to fade but can also cause deterioration in the structure of the fibres themselves.

Another enemy to textiles is atmospheric pollution and, despite clean-air zones, the sulphur dioxide content in the air continues to harm textiles in industrial and urban areas and all other places where vehicles still emit their destructive fumes. Any kind of dust and dirt can be harmful, particularly if the dirt contains gritty particles which can work their way into fabrics and cut the fibres.

Excessive dryness and heat, damp which can rot fibres or cause mould to grow, pests such as moths and insects, chemical reactions set up by the constituents of stains and starches and their interaction with each other – all these can attack fibres and weaken them.

3 *Figure in a Gothic tapestry of the sixteenth century before conservation. Much of the dark wool of the outlines has fallen out.*

4 *The same figure after conservation. The replacement of the dark outlines has greatly improved the delineation.*

Up to now we have mentioned external conditions but a textile can have inherent weakness caused in manufacturing which might result in its destruction. Some dyeing processes, although achieving the desired shade, will weaken and eventually cause the destruction of fibres. An example of this is the rotting by oxidation of the dark-coloured wools in tapestries. Before the existence of chemical dyes, iron was used as a mordant to obtain dark colours, particularly black and brown. More recent restoration work has shown that the dark outlines in the design, typical of Gothic tapestries of the sixteenth century, have had to be renewed on several previous occasions. But recent conservation replacement of these outlines, so vital for the proper visual appreciation of the design, with wools dyed by modern methods, should

ensure that replacements will not be needed so frequently in the future.

The detrimental effects of dyeing methods do not apply only in the case of old textiles. Starch dyes may well have been used on some of the present-day textiles which holidaymakers bring as souvenirs from abroad. The bright and beautiful colours which attract travellers could disappear or run if the materials are either washed, kept in humid conditions or exposed to light, and therefore the materials need to be kept clean, dry and in the dark if they are to survive.

The late eighteenth and early nineteenth centuries saw a transition as far as dyeing was concerned because the earlier natural dyes were being replaced by chemical dyes. A great deal of experimentation took place and, consequently, the dyestuffs used were not always completely

5 *Tattered fragments of a historically important regimental colour are preserved by couching onto a suitable backing fabric. Enlargement shows the technique used.*

successful. Some were so fugitive that they would bleed their colour into surrounding areas just by exposure to damp atmosphere, let alone by being put in water. There is one green colour, very much used at one time for embroidery silks, which is a great culprit in this respect. We remember a man's beautifully embroidered silk waistcoat, obviously never worn, which had unfortunately been stored in damp conditions and was almost completely ruined because of this particular colour running. On a piece of canvas-work embroidery a brown dye had actually rotted the fibres of the canvas on which the embroidery was worked, to the extent that the parts embroidered in brown had fallen out, although leaving enough traces to show the reason for the disintegration. It is interesting, from a historical point of view, that aniline dyes seem to have been discovered before the man-made materials on which they are most effective and permanent. Aniline dyes began to be used about the middle of the last century on various textiles, but it may be that their true potential has not yet been realised and that they may have more affinity with man-made fibres now being perfected than they had on natural ones, on which they were apt to fade and change.

Manufacturing processes or finishes, too, can do long-term harm as a result of distortion or chemical treatment of the fibres even though, when new, the material is attractive and pleasing. An illustration of this is the weighting of silk previously mentioned. It is likely that weighting of some kind has been known from the beginning of the silk industry in China, and a small amount of the weighting agent may not appreciably affect the lasting qualities of silk, whether woven or used for embroidery. However, from about 1870 weighting began to be done excessively. Although some companies did little or no weighting, one firm stated in 1909 that coloured silks could be weighted to between fifty and one hundred per cent and black silk up to four to five hundred per cent. For heavy weighting, the silk could be kept for days in a bath with tin or iron salts. Garments made of new weighted silk have the scroop, or rustle in movement, which was so fashionably desirable, besides having a heavy and expensive feel. Fringes and tassels too, hang much better if the silk from which they are made has been weighted.

Weighting makes silk more susceptible to damage from light and, over a period of time, the weakened fibres of weighted silk tend to split and break, especially along the folds and hems where there is already some stress. These splits are indicative of a general weakness in the material and it is very difficult to do anything to save it. Other dressings and manufacturing processes may also hasten deterioration, whichever fibres have been used, but silk in particular has always been subjected to many different finishing processes.

If two different fibres are woven together into a material, one may actually contribute to the destruction of the other. Although both wool and silk will tolerate a degree of moisture and, indeed, wool actually needs moisture to survive, silk will rot if allowed to remain damp. A material woven with a mixture of silk and wool yarns may look and feel most attractive but will not last long in damp conditions.

Conservation of textiles

Considering everything, it is a wonder that textiles survive for any length of time at all, and yet Britain is particularly rich in textiles of historic importance, some of considerable age. Many, of course, are in museums where they can be kept in controlled conditions and, as more is known and understood about conservation methods and techniques, this should ensure that they are safe for future generations to see and study. Other historic textiles are in more open conditions, many in country houses, often in the very surroundings for which they were originally made. Their future is less certain, but there is an increasing awareness of the dangers and an acceptance of the responsibility for their maintenance on the part of those who have to care for them. Still other textiles are in private ownership, valued as family heirlooms, or purchased because they appealed as decorative objects or as additions to a collection. There may be others packed away, half-remembered or even forgotten.

A textile does not need to look old and worn to need care. Prevention is always better than cure, and preventive conservation is an important and positive way to ensure that a treasured piece in good condition will remain so, whether it is on display or in storage.

If a textile requires treatment of any kind, then it will be necessary to decide who should be entrusted with the work. This is the first and most important decision to be made. At the risk of labouring the point, textiles of historic or artistic importance should be treated only by an experienced textile conservator. So much can go wrong, and treatment by a well-meaning but inexperienced person could do irreparable harm.

How can anyone decide if a piece is important? If its history is not known already, the owner should find out as much about it as possible. Research could first be done at libraries, local museums or branches of the Embroiderers' Guild. It could also be taken or sent to the Victoria & Albert Museum for appraisal. It is necessary to write or phone first for an appointment; the department to contact is the Textile Department or, if the piece is Oriental, the Far Eastern or Indian Department. They will want to know what the textile object is – e.g. embroidery, costume, a piece of canvas-work, woven tapestry, lace – so that the appropriate expert will be seen who will be able to give information about the textile, its use and date and its importance but who will not, of course, be able to value it. The museum does give a postal advisory service, but that means sending the textile by registered post and there is always a delay of about a month before it is returned, so a visit is preferable. If a valuation is required then application should be made to one of the well-known auctioneers and valuers. If you own a collectable piece and wish to sell it, then it is best to do so before it receives any treatment so that the new owner can decide whether he wishes it to be conserved or restored and to whom he will take it for treatment.

A piece does not have to be spectacular to be important, but its age and rarity may give it historic or artistic significance.

There are still some quite important textiles around, not all of them immediately recognisable as such; perhaps a few examples of previously unknown but valuable pieces which have come our way may be of interest.

Two orphreys

First of all two orphreys, pieces of ecclesiastical embroidery in silk and metal threads closely covering a linen background, were brought to us for cleaning. The first piece in the form of a cross was rather out of shape and the other, a straight piece, showed some signs of wear. They were dirty but in good condition. We felt that they were of an early date, even though they had, we were told, been recently removed from a vest-

ment of purple Victorian velvet, possibly the last of many vestments they had decorated.

The Victoria & Albert Museum confirmed our assessment and identified them as examples of Opus Anglicanum, dated about 1425, and the experts were even fairly certain from their style in which professional workshop they had been made. The quality of the materials used was excellent, as would have been expected from professional work of that time. This, and the fact that the pieces had been revered and therefore handled carefully, had undoubtedly contributed to their survival in such good condition. The small amount of damage on the straight piece had probably happened because that piece had been used to decorate the front of the vestment, and had therefore been subjected to rubbing when the priest's garment had brushed against the altar, a common cause of damage to altar frontals and the fronts of vestments.

Cleaned and straightened, with the laid goldwork background gleaming softly, the silk embroidery showing the delicate shading of the saint's robes and the moulding of the figure on the cross in the centre, there was no question that here was something beautiful, of artistic as well as historic importance. Nothing was taken from or added to the pieces and no attempt made to mend them; responsible conservation seeks to save what is there. The orphreys are now kept safe in a museum with a controlled environment, to be enjoyed as fine examples of early English work.

Embroidered linen

The second example was a piece of embroidered linen brought to us for cleaning, mounting and framing. It was about 14×10 in (36×25 cm), a piece of coarse linen on which animals and insects were embroidered in tent stitch. The piece was dirty and some of the threads of the linen background were broken. The animals and the insects were placed in a haphazard fashion, rather widely spaced, and with no apparent attempt at a balanced design. Nevertheless, the piece had an artless charm which had prompted the owner to buy it at a fête. Research showed that its date was about 1600.

6 *Opus Anglicanum embroidery; the back panel of a chasuble. Dated about 1425. Now in the Royal Ontario Museum, Toronto, Canada.*

7 *Vertical band of Opus Anglicanum embroidery – the front panel of the chasuble, showing signs of wear from rubbing. Now in the Royal Ontario Museum, Toronto, Canada.*

8 *Detail of a piece of Elizabethan sprigs embroidery before conservation. Already backed with similar linen to which it will be attached, with a minimum of stitching around the broken areas and pins through stronger parts to hold it in position.*

There are samplers of Elizabethan work with similar embroidered animals or insects where a snail or a butterfly is the same size as a frog or even a lion, as if all the creatures were felt to be of equal importance, but in samplers the placing of the animals does have a balance and design, and generally they are quite close together. Elizabethan needlewomen often applied motifs, already embroidered on linen or fine canvas, onto rich background materials. Any visitor to Hardwick Hall in Derbyshire will have seen examples of this and it could be that these motifs were sometimes sold already embroidered. Whether this piece was an example of such work we do not know, but it is an interesting theory. The piece itself was washed, supported on another piece of

9 *Detail shown in figure 8 after conservation.*

linen, made safe, mounted and framed. It looked charming. There is still research which could be done on it but, again, nothing has been added or taken away and if, later someone wishes to find out more, the owner has an up-to-date report on

10 *Back view of the completed piece showing the remarkably small amount of stitching required to make the piece safe and tidy.*

11 *The completed piece mounted for framing.*

our findings and on what has been done in the way of treatment.

A double-woven petticoat

Other finds were items of dress bought by a collector, the first being a petticoat dated about 1740 and which, at first sight, seemed similar to others of the period. It was made of quilted cream satin in a very pleasant design. Examined in more detail, however, there was found to be no seam stitching the lining in place between the top part of the petticoat, which was fitted into the waistband, and the quilted part below. Closer examination revealed that the garment was made up of several widths of a double-woven fabric, joined together with vertical seams. The top part of each width was made of the two weaves 'tied' together in a single layer of material. In the lower section the two weaves were only joined in the outlines of the design and the quilted effect had been achieved by the weaver adding a filler weft of padding in the course of weaving. This method of producing a material which had only one thickness for that part of the petticoat nearest the waist and hips, with the lower part of the garment padded, must have made the petticoat very flexible and comfortable to wear, and very warm too. This example of double weaving including padding is, as far as we have been able to ascertain, unique in Britain. The petticoat was carefully photographed and documented and will continue to be of great interest to both weavers and students of the history of costume.

12 *Petticoat – weaving simulating quilting. Now in exhibition of costume in the collection of Charles Stewart at Shambellie House, in Scotland.*

Two pairs of trousers

The last find concerned two pairs of blue and white striped trousers, eventually identified as early and rare examples of sailor's uniform of the period of the Napoleonic wars. The clothes of ordinary working people are seldom found in costume collections. There are many reasons for this. Made initially of materials of inferior quality, such clothes are usually discarded when worn out or else cut down for other uses and seldom survive. Uniforms for ordinary seamen are comparatively recent. Naval ratings originally had to supply their own working clothes, but these trousers were probably specially provided and are therefore historically important. One pair is now in the National Maritime Museum and the other in the Royal Albert Memorial Museum in Exeter. The trousers could not be dated with absolute accuracy but even that might have been possible had we known in time that the chemical composition of tar had been changed at a certain date. The trousers had unsightly tar marks, which were removed; had they been analysed first, this might have helped to date the trousers a little

13 *Detail of lower part of the petticoat. Quilted effect seen from the right side.*

14 *Enlarged detail of the same area on the wrong (reverse) side showing how the filling was incorporated during the actual weaving.*

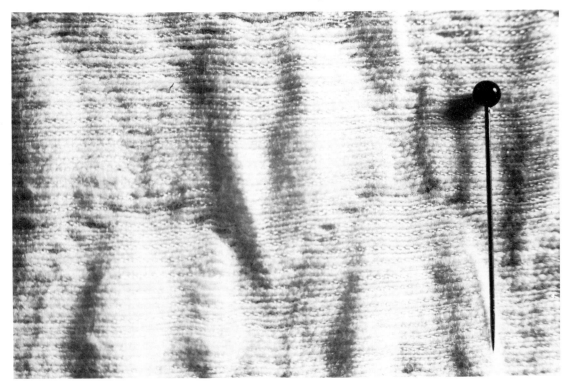

more closely. This demonstrates that the removal of stains from historical textiles is not always a wise or proper course to take, apart from considerations of the possible damage to the old textile. The ethics of responsible conservation hold that nothing of the original shall be removed and nothing added, unless it is necessary to make the object safe or visually understandable; however, if stains can be removed safely, they are not generally left unless they themselves are important. Thus bloodstains on garments of a historically important person should not be removed.

The examples we have given of textiles which were proved to be important can, of course, be matched by others where, far from geese turning into swans, the opposite was the case.

A canvas-work panel

A canvas-work panel worked in *gros-point* and *petit-point* was acquired at auction and brought for treatment. It certainly had the appearance of a seventeenth-century piece and the new owner was delighted with her bargain. Close examination of the canvas and wools, however, pointed to a French nineteenth-century origin, although the style and subject was seventeenth century. It was impossible to prove conclusively without lengthy research whether it was a copy or just an example of something done in an earlier style. The materials were not very good and the work necessary to make it safe made it very much less of a bargain than had at first seemed the case, although it was still a pleasant piece of work.

A framed tapestry

Our last example concerns a fairly large framed tapestry which had hung for many years in the bar of an inn. It had gradually become very dark from the tobacco smoke in the atmosphere until a visitor, viewing it through the haze, suggested that it appeared to be of a very fine weave, in good general condition, and that it might be valuable and should be cleaned.

It was brought for treatment and proved to be not, as the owners had hoped, a fine, hand-

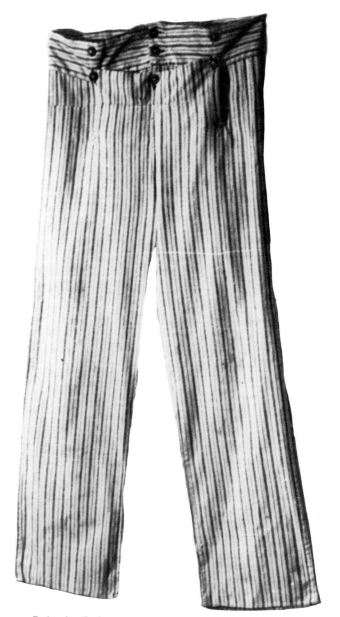

15 *Pair of sailor's trousers.*

woven woollen tapestry, but a very good, cotton, machine-made imitation. Imitations of both woven tapestries and canvas-work embroideries were very effectively machine-made in the nineteenth century, and are important as a tribute to man's ingenuity rather than his artistry. We also explained that, as dry-cleaning would have made little or no improvement to its appearance and, thus, that it would have to be washed, the piece would almost certainly shrink, being cotton and not wool, and it would then need a new, smaller frame. The owners decided not to have the work done and it is quite possible that they put it back on to the pub wall to grow even darker and more mysterious.

Caring and preserving textiles means having a responsible attitude towards them. Expert treatment may be expensive and, from a purely mercenary point of view, may hardly make financial sense; the cost of the work necessary may well be greater than the market value of the textile, even after conservation. If research and expert assessment reveals that the textile is of less importance, however much it means to the owner, then that may justify the owner undertaking any necessary treatment personally.

The first step should be to record the results of research and advice and, later, to record any treatment given, and to keep this documentation safely.

If a professional undertakes conservation or restoration work, the owner should have a detailed report accompanying the textile when it is returned. This documentation is important should anyone have to treat the textile again in the future.

Ideally, the same sort of documentation should be kept by any person undertaking textile conservation, together with the results of any research undertaken and a photographic record of work done.

2

Volunteers and conservation

We are not all capable of everything
Virgil, *Eclogues*

Caring people in any circumstances, having become aware of a need, take action to offer help. Thus when textiles, particularly those in historic houses open to the public, show signs of deterioration and an obvious need for remedial treatment, those who care about textiles and feel themselves competent to give help, volunteer to do so either as individuals or members of some organisation.

Ironically, as we have explained elsewhere, the deteriorated condition of the textiles is often the direct result of opening the houses to the public.

The acceptance of voluntary help poses problems; not all immediately obvious. For instance, it is not always easy to channel enthusiasm and what the volunteer force is prepared and able to do in terms of time, skill and length of commitment into ways which will answer the actual need and also be cost effective.

Unfortunately it does not always become immediately apparent that, though the help offered is classed as voluntary, it is extremely unlikely that no cost will be involved. There will be the cost of any materials and equipment and possibly too the travelling expenses of the variable workforce.

From experience, we would advise very careful forward planning and the setting out of clear guidelines for obtaining agreements on areas of responsibility, so that everyone is made aware, from the outset, of what will be involved in terms of commitments in both time and cost before embarking on any scheme.

It is wise to collect as much information as possible from intending volunteers so that full advantage may be taken of the differing skills of those who wish to participate and, most importantly, of the time they wish to give.

Similarly, the owner or custodian of the textiles should be quite specific about the exact nature of the help needed.

In the early stages, a meeting of all intending volunteers should be called, at which a trained and qualified textile conservator could talk and answer questions. The Textile Conservation Centre's Information Sheet No. 4 (Oct. 1977) sets out what is relevant to making good use of voluntary help and is reproduced in its entirety at the back of this book.

The methods of carrying out the preventive conservation measures suggested are explained in Chapter 4, but practical work with which volunteers can assist in the good housekeeping techniques necessary to keep safe the textiles in a house open to the public will be successful only if such work is properly organised to an arranged schedule, agreed and accepted by all concerned and carried out without fail.

For instance, if someone is unable to attend to an allotted task, provision should exist so that a substitute will take over the responsibility.

Those volunteers who are unable to make firm commitments may still make valuable contributions by going on the stand-by list, or by undertaking work where they are free to vary their attendance, such as fund raising, which can take many forms, from maintaining regular contact with contributors to helping in occasional bursts of activity in fund-raising events.

Research and documentation can move at the researcher's pace, involving visits to libraries or museums for the purpose of recording the collections of the house itself.

Every volunteer should be able to make a worthwhile contribution at some level. What is essential is organisation, and honesty on both sides – from the volunteer on the amount of time and effort available, and from the organisers by a clear indication of what is needed.

If conditions or initial promises cannot be maintained, then this must be made clear as soon as possible so that no-one among the group or the organisers and, especially, no historic textile, suffers in any way.

The area in which volunteers most often offer to help is in actual conservation treatment to the textiles. The attraction of being able to save a priceless piece of textile history, can be readily understood, but this is not something which should be undertaken lightly either by owners or volunteers.

Apart from possible damage to the textiles themselves, other factors need careful consideration. Conservation projects in which volunteers can give the greatest help are those requiring a great deal of repetitive work on large textiles important enough to warrant the enormous number of hours of work needed to save them; work, of course, which must be done to a consistently high standard. The advantage of using voluntary workers is of no consequence if the work takes too long to cover the overheads which, even given rent-free accommodation, is usually about a quarter of the cost of professional work, because then the voluntary labour becomes a liability in economic terms.

The only practical advantage of using volunteers for remedial conservation work is when the sheer scale of the project, in terms of time and labour being tied up in it, would have made acceptance of the job by a professional workroom extremely doubtful.

The basic necessities of setting up a successful conservation treatment project manned by volunteers are:

1 the employment of a full-time trained and qualified textile conservator to supervise the work

2 suitable premises – secure, properly heated, lit and furnished with the correct equipment and materials

3 facilities in the area for a hand basin, kitchen, lavatory and somewhere away from the work where food can be eaten

4 staff to keep the premises clean

The cost of running the workroom will include the salary of the supervising conservator, overhead expenses of the room, materials and equipment, general administrative costs, volunteers' travelling expenses and the provision of insurance in case of accidents to any of the personnel involved, or damage to the objects or premises.

No voluntary workforce will be readily available unless the workroom is set in a good catchment area from which a pool of skilled and responsible volunteers can be recruited and replenished whenever the need arises.

If this sounds formidable it is, but it can, and does, work. The setting up of the National Trust's workroom at Knole House in Kent, was instigated by Karen Finch in 1974 after she had carried out a survey of the textiles at Knole for the Trust. In her report she stated that the conservation of the rare and beautiful textiles of the King's Bed and the coverings of the chairs, stools and cushions en suite with it presented an almost overwhelming challenge in sheer scale, but that the need for action was extremely urgent if these important textiles were to be preserved.

Having researched and perfected a suitable method of conservation, the problem was reduced to being able to recruit personnel to do the repetitive work to a consistently high standard. At the initial meeting in September 1974 a large number of volunteers filled in specially prepared forms which supplied data for assessing the skills and time offered, and planning went ahead while the National Trust's staff at Knole prepared the workroom.

An article by John Cornforth in *Country Life* (25 November, 1982) considers in some detail textile conservation at Knole and other historic houses, the work of volunteers and, in particular, the actual cost of textile conservation in this country, the continuing need for it and the difficulties of funding the work already done and still needing to be done.

The final thought we would like to leave concerns potential damage that volunteers may unwittingly cause if they go ahead with actual treatment without the safeguard of professional advice and guidance. Unless one has had proper training in textile conservation, it is difficult to envisage all the possibilities of damage inherent in carrying out what can seem a quite simple and straightforward treatment.

The immediate result of treatment may seem satisfactory but damage, once caused, whether immediate or delayed, can never be reversed, even by the most skilful professional conservator. Such damage will not only have ruined the piece but will also have destroyed for ever any important evidence it could have yielded to future scholarly research.

3

Colour

Beauty is in the eye of the beholder
Margaret Hungerford, *Molly Brawn*

Providing that no attempt is made to deceive by any alteration or replacement during conservation treatment, the fragmented remains of a textile can be presented quite ethically in such a way as to appear more whole than is actually the case, and to allow those who view it to have an understanding of its original size, shape and appearance.

Such visual impressions can be created by the informed choice of colour and texture in the materials used to present the object after conservation treatment, during which nothing will have been removed which might contain evidence of the past, so vital for future research, nor anything added which might deceive with false evidence, thus destroying the authenticity of the piece as an historical document.

Understanding colour and the effects of what it conveys is essential for all who study, design and create new textiles and for those who seek to preserve textile objects by conservation. Evidence of the symbolic significance of colours can be found throughout history, particularly in religious observance.

Colour symbolism is universally understood today – for example, red for danger, yellow for caution and green for safety. The different colours of uniforms, flags and banners identify groups or nations, and there is worldwide understanding of white offering truce or surrender. In conservation or in designing new work, the choosing of colours requires an understanding of the basic principles of visual colour. The colour circle we have chosen to explain these principles will, we hope, be of value to conservators and as an exercise in seeing. Each of the three primary colours, red, blue and yellow has a complementary colour made up by a mixture of the other two colours. This fact becomes evident if one stares at one of the primary colours until it appears to have a halo of light and then transfers one's gaze to a plain white background, when the complementary colour of that primary colour will appear to be reflected.

The complementary colour of red is green, made from blue and yellow; the complementary colour of blue is orange, made from yellow and red, and the complementary colour of yellow is violet, made from red and blue.

The circle takes form when the three complementary colours are each placed opposite their primary colours and then they become known as secondary colours. The six colours now in the circle may be referred to as pure colours. By mixing neighbouring colours together in equal proportions a further six colours are achieved which, again, will prove to be opposite their complementary colours in the circle.

In nature it will be seen that if an object is predominantly red, its shadow will be mainly green in composition, while areas of light with yellow hues throw violet shadows and blue objects produce orange shadows.

Closely adjacent complementary colours appear to strengthen each other and become more intense when viewed at close quarters, but this effect disappears at a distance in proportion to the diminished size of the area of each colour.

This colour circle may be developed into a twelve-pointed star in order to demonstrate what happens visually as the coloured areas get smaller and closer and appear to mix with each other.

Before the colours finally cancel each other out by proximity with their opposites in the circle, they become greyer and duller in appearance the further the distance from which they are viewed, until they turn into a muddy brown by uniting in the middle of the star shape.

An important consideration when dealing with colour is that reds, oranges and yellows are known as warm colours which appear to move towards us, while colours grouped around blue are cold colours which appear to recede from us.

This effect is used by painters to suggest perspective. It is also one of the main reasons why restoring or copying works of art is so difficult, as even infinitesimal and hardly observable changes in colour values can make a crucial difference to the perspective of any design, and particularly to pictorial design.

Black and white, yellow-green and red-violet are known as neutral colours – neither warm nor cool – though any colour may be made to appear warmer or cooler by putting a more extreme colour next to it. By making use of these qualities, warm colours may be used to promote sensations of warmth and well-being while cool colours may convey sensations of cold and dislike. The sensation evoked by the various yellow shades is a reminder of sunshine, while blue is a reminder of cold and ice. Neutral yellow-green is felt as restful, while red in large amounts tends to excite; too much purple or violet can be depressing – and yet all these sensations can be offset by the way the colours are balanced with each other.

The pigments or dyestuffs that produce the primary colours may be found in nearly pure form in nature, but the development and use of colour and dyes has always been complex and of interest to scientists as well as to artists and dyers and has, in various civilisations, been seen as both mysterious and of great commercial value in trading.

Colour and light
All colours agree in the dark
Francis Bacon, *Essays*

It is said that persons with normal colour vision can distinguish 200,000 colour nuances or shades. However, to make proper use of this facility it is necessary to take into account the fact that colour and light are indivisible, and that the sensation of seeing colour is the result of the interpretation by the central nervous system of the effect produced upon the eye by electromagnetic radiation of a particular wavelength.

How colour is perceived depends on a number of different factors, including the fact that only the middle part of the electromagnetic waves which make up the spectrum are visible to the human eye. The light waves outside our vision are the ultra-violet waves on one side and the infra-red waves at the other end of the band or beam.

We see light either directly from its source i.e. the sun or a lamp, or indirectly from an object reflecting or absorbing this light. If light waves go through an object, as with glass, we see that object as colourless since no colour is reflected from it. Colour is defined by the eye itself and results from the fact that a material or an object will, depending on its physical properties, reflect or absorb certain wavelengths of the light that strikes it. If violet, blue, green, yellow and orange waves are the ones mainly absorbed by the object and the red waves are reflected, then the object will be perceived as red. Some objects, such as mirrors, reflect nearly all the light that reaches them in accordance with the quality of that light.

Colour and conservation

New snow reflects most of the light that strikes it and white painted walls may reflect up to 75 per cent of any light while, incidentally, absorbing the greater number of ultra violet waves.

Colour reflects light according to its intensity or depth of shade, with pale colours reflecting more light than darker colours. Smooth, untwisted silk filaments and fine satin-woven silk will appear glossy by reflecting light, while the shadows thrown by woollen yarns or plain woven woollen fabric will absorb light in proportion to the relative roughness of the yarns involved.

Colours appear stronger and more defined when underlined by shadows because the colour waves reflected from an even smoothness are contrasted by those absorbed by unevenness. Since the shadows contain the absorbed part of the spectrum, they form the complementary colours to the ones reflected. Hence the colours of woollen yarns appear to affect their neighbours more than the colours of silk, which are mainly reflected, thereby acquiring a glossy shine which, in itself, tends to baffle our vision.

Consequently, each coloured modern yarn put into the conservation of a tapestry woven predominately from woollen fibres, which absorb the light, will affect the colour of its surroundings. This fact adds to the difficulties of matching new colours to old, especially when introducing different types of dyestuffs with differing characteristics from that of the type used originally.

Each dyestuff will inevitably fade or change according to its own built-in rules, and so any restoration will eventually show up, first under special lighting and, in the course of time, under any form of lighting. The time factor is dependent on whether the textile which has received repair, e.g. a tapestry, is kept under climatically controlled conditions or displayed in open conditions, as would be the case in a historic house.

The nuance of shading in alien materials used in a supportive role in the treatment of an old textile might be less critical were it not for the fact that light reflects differently from differing angles and from different types of dyestuffs and fabrics.

Conservation, as opposed to restoration, makes less use of alien material and thereby gives fewer opportunities for changes to take place. In the long term this makes conservation of tapestries of greater aesthetic value because the pictorial quality of the tapestries will sustain less damage and the underlying draughtsmanship will be less impaired too. Even a relatively small area of restoration or reconstruction which has subsequently changed colour becomes very obvious even at a glance, and can be visually disturbing and detract from the appreciation of the tapestry as a whole.

Colour and display

In choosing a fabric to support a fragile textile as part of its conservation treatment, careful consideration must be given to the weight, texture and especially the colour of the supporting fabric, so that in every way it unobtrusively enhances as well as gives support. As a general rule it will be found to be more satisfactory to use darker rather than lighter colours, because this appears to intensify the colour of the supported textile. A similar effect is often obtained by using a dark blue or grey mount in framing.

To obtain uniformity in seeing colours, we have been conditioned to aim at producing daylight condition though we must, of necessity, accept that daylight itself is a constantly changing commodity. Tungsten light is, in fact, more flattering and transmits fewer ultra violet waves.

Since the light reflection from different types of dyestuff is so variable, the use of any material with dyestuffs alien to it could cause undesirable changes in its appearance.

To choose colours for supporting fabrics and for the interior of cases in which to display objects to their best advantage after conservation, it might prove worthwhile to construct a light-box containing different kinds of artificial light sources. The use of such a light-box for demonstrations while planning an exhibition could also lead to rewarding discussions between exhibition designers, conservators and curators. Even someone with only one object to display should decide on the best colour for mount, frame and general surroundings in both daylight and artificial light before making a final decision.

Using the many facets of colour has occupied artists and designers for a very long time and is obviously an area which should not be overlooked by conservators and curators intent on conserving objects by the simplest means possible, including enhancing the look of any object without interference with the object itself but by considered choice of colour for support and display.

Consider how the colour of most objects is improved when seen on a background of a muted blue shade, remember that smooth uncreased textiles reflect more light and therefore look cleaner than do crumpled pieces; add these two factors to the many others which can enhance the appearance of an object and it will be recognised that, though beauty may be in the eye of the beholder, it is nearly always possible to influence the beholder to see what he is intended to see.

Using the power of symbolism with a working knowledge of the rules governing colour and light should help in displaying fragile objects safely and, in particular, achieving the goal of sound preventive conservation, which is to create the least possible interference with objects of cultural importance while still making them appear right for the purpose of their exhibition.

4

Display and preventive conservation

The stately homes of England,
How beautiful they stand!
Felicia Hemans, *The Homes of England*

If one possesses, or has in one's care, something beautiful and visually satisfying, then it is natural to want to look at and enjoy it and, of course, allow others to share that pleasure. This can be achieved by putting the object in an accessible position and, one would think, in a good light. But, if the object is a textile, a great deal of further thought is required. Light, especially its ultra violet radiation, is harmful to textiles, causing fading of colour and alteration in the structure of the fibres, resulting in disintegration; observe how quickly the material of curtains at a sunny window can deteriorate. Obviously, then, the amount and intensity of light in the place chosen for the display of the textile will be of the greatest importance.

Light

The international unit of illumination is the lux. For example in Britain, in summer, direct sunlight out of doors could measure as much as 100,000 lux, and the measurement on a dull day, inside would be about 600 lux. From a conservation point of view, the advocated illumination for textiles is no more than 50 lux. In the open conditions of a house as opposed to the more controlled ones of a museum, some compromise regarding the exposure of textiles to light must be achieved, but very fragile pieces should be displayed where light can be excluded whenever it is possible to do so. These pieces should always be kept well away from direct light with, possibly, a well-placed source of artificial light

for occasional use, remembering that artificial light can also cause damage. Filters for absorbing ultra violet rays can be obtained in sheets or as a varnish for application to windows. The effective life of these filters is limited, so obtain instruction from the manufacturers regarding frequency of renewal for continued safety. Ordinary electric light bulbs and tungsten incandescent lighting are safer than fluorescent, which should be avoided as it is liable to emit ultra violet rays unless filters are fitted.

Protective housekeeping

There are other ways to show care for textiles on open display. Valuable lessons can be learned from the way that the good housekeeping techniques of the past have preserved textiles in many of the great houses of Britain, where tapestries, curtains, bedhangings, furniture and carpets of great age can still be seen, often in the very surroundings for which they were originally made. Many of the houses are situated in the clean air of country parkland, away from the air pollution of industry, but that would not have been sufficient reason for the survival of the textiles, although it would have helped. Far more important is the treatment that the textiles and, indeed, all the contents of the houses received in the past.

It was customary for the staff to be instructed to keep the furniture fitted with loose covers even when the family was in residence, and we know from eighteenth-century writers that these covers were removed only for the visit of someone of the greatest importance. Treasured bed hangings had their own sets of protective covers, entire carpets were normally protected by coverings of baize or drugget, or strips of drugget were laid over those areas of carpet where the greatest wear could be expected. Even in quite humble homes, strips of hardwearing floor covering were laid over parts of the carpets to take the tread. It was also the general custom to draw the blinds of all windows against sunlight, especially those of important rooms, to save carpets, covers and furniture from fading. In a great house, when the family were not in residence, everything was protected. Drugget was laid over all the carpets, dust-sheets covered the furniture and the blinds were drawn down.

Protective housekeeping of this kind is textile conservation in its simplest and most effective form. It meant, of course, that the owners of those beautiful textiles rarely enjoyed their possessions, and one must hope that they were satisfied with the pride of ownership and the knowledge that they could, if they wished, gaze upon their treasures at any time. By their care, they have left a very important record of how great houses were furnished and decorated. Unfortunately, even before many of the houses were opened to the public, it had become difficult for subsequent owners to maintain those early high standards of care because of the dwindling number of staff available, and many of the textiles had already begun to suffer.

The presence of visitors in large numbers can contribute substantially to the deterioration of textiles and deterioration is a process which accelerates very rapidly. Opening a house to the public means subjecting the contents to increased exposure to light and to constant changes in temperature and humidity, all of which harm textiles. Those responsible for the care of the contents of such houses have a very real problem in trying to achieve a fair balance of interests so that visitors may enjoy the textiles without making too great a contribution to their destruction.

But even allowing for the fact that visitors will wish to see the textiles, there are still some safeguards in the way of preventive conservation which can be taken. Blinds should always be drawn down and the light excluded in every possible way when there are no visitors. Even when the houses are open, it is possible to cut down the amount of light, particularly sunlight, which is allowed to enter the rooms, while still allowing sufficient illumination for the rooms to be viewed in comfort; in fact, many objects can be seen better in a subdued light. The human eye is very adaptable and, provided the change is gradual, can see in a surprisingly small amount of light. It would be possible, therefore, to decrease the amount of light available as the visitors proceed along a defined route through the house, say towards a corridor with no daylight at all. Here, fragile textile objects could be displayed in conditions where the minimum amount of artificial light was available for adequate viewing without causing visual discomfort or a feeling that the lighting was insufficient. Some museums solve the problem by using low general lighting and intermittent spot-lighting, again of surprisingly low power, so that very precious and fragile objects are exposed to the least possible light, and this method could be employed to some extent in other situations.

Atmospheric conditions
I durst not laugh for fear of opening my lips and receiving the bad air Shakespeare, *Julius Caesar*

A constant temperature of 13°–14°C (55°–57°F), with a relative humidity of 50–60 per cent, is considered ideal for textiles. Unfortunately, little can be done to eliminate the fluctuations of temperature and humidity in a house open to the public without incurring prohibitive expense as well as altering the general setting. Putting individual items or groups of items into air-conditioned display cases for safety could alter the appearance of the rooms and create the feeling of being in a museum rather than a home.

The air-conditioning of whole rooms could mean their being closed to the public, who would then be obliged to view them either from the outside or by some special arrangement inside the rooms. In either case, the great charm and attraction of being able to walk around in a house and sense the atmosphere would be lost.

In a private house, however, an owner is able to choose the position of a textile and can regulate the amount of light, the temperature and the humidity. The use of a dimly-lit corridor as a place for displaying textile pictures and hangings is worth consideration, as is the use of low-powered artificial light with ultra violet filters.

Textile collections

A serious collector of textile objects has special problems of display and storage relating to his own particular interest and, if the collection is valuable, there is also the question of security. It is wise to keep a good colour photograph and detailed description of each piece in a safe place away from the collection. For actual display, it might be worthwhile to provide a small, secure area with good, safe conditions as regarding light, temperature and humidity, and to show only a few items at a time, varying the display at intervals from a main collection which could remain safe in storage but be easily accessible both for reference and the examination by fellow collectors when required. An index or good labelling system will facilitate easy identification in storage. Provided that the alteration of the display does not entail a great deal of handling, the objects would benefit from less exposure to light and the outside atmosphere, and from the period of rest that good storage facilities provide.

Mounting textiles for framing

Smaller and more fragile textiles, for example embroidered pictures, pieces of lace or samplers, are more safely displayed by being mounted behind glass in a frame. The first essential is that the textile should be clean and it is quite possible that it may also require some support or repair before being mounted. How to carry out these processes is explained in later chapters but, for the moment, we will assume

16 *Back of an old stretcher frame after removal of the canvas-work picture.*

that the piece is clean and strong.

In the past, the normal method of mounting a textile for framing seems to have been to attach it with tacks to a wooden stretcher which was like a rough frame, as most people who take an old textile from its frame will find, although occasionally the textile was simply backed with a piece of cardboard. The wood of a stretcher might have warped due to changes in humidity, and this will have altered the tension on the textile. The tacks holding the fabric to the stretcher are often found to have caused damage by rusting and rotting the fibres, or by cutting into and breaking them. Moreover, wood which becomes damp will stain any material with which it comes into contact, and this has often been the case if there has been a supporting piece across the stretcher in a rather large fabric picture. Most old frames will be found to have allowed a great deal of dust and damp to enter and the centre of a fabric mounted on a stretcher will almost certainly have become very dusty. In short, experience gained in seeing the long-term effects of this way of framing textiles has prompted us to advocate another method which gives the textile greater all-over support and affords better protection against the damaging effects of damp and dust.

It is not advisable to use cardboard as a mount

18 *Canvas-work picture after conservation and reframing with a suitable mount and frame.*

17 *Canvas-work picture removed from frame and showing damage from tacks and accumulated dust.*

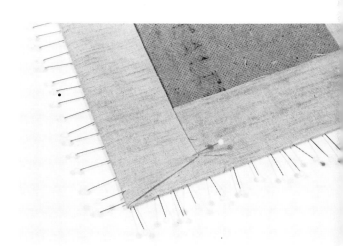

19 *Covering hardboard with linen – back of hardboard. The pins assure correct positioning before sticking linen to the hardboard on the back only.*

as this might contain an acid harmful to textiles and is also liable to absorb moisture. More suitable is a piece of hardboard which has been cut to size very slightly larger than the area of the textile which it is intended to show when in the frame. The hardboard is then covered with a piece of linen or similar material made from natural fibres, cut about 3 in (8 cm) larger on all sides than the hardboard. The linen is placed over the smooth surface of the hardboard, absolutely straight, and then stretched taut and fixed by turning the extra material on each side over to the rough back of the hardboard and

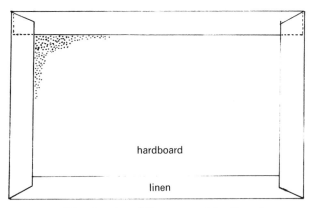

20 *Line drawing of linen-covered hardboard mount as seen from the back.*

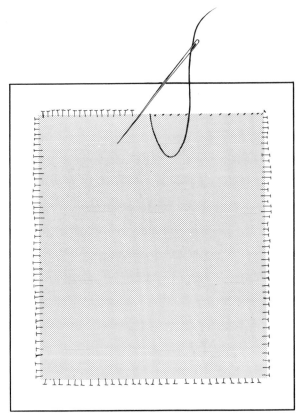

21 *Textile being stitched to linen-covered hardboard mount, with stitches taking over from very carefully placed pins.*

sticking it down with a polyvinyl acetate adhesive, taking care not to allow any of the adhesive to get on to the front or the edges of the hardboard. The corners of the linen should be trimmed so that, when the sticking is done, there is as smooth a finish as possible. It is important that the threads of the linen are straight in both directions and that the linen is stretched taut across the front of the hardboard. The linen-covered hardboard should then be put under weights to give the adhesive 24 hours to dry thoroughly before mounting the clean textile.

Starting at the top, pin the centred textile to the edge of the linen on the hardboard, making sure that the edge of the textile is as straight as possible. Remember that pins, like needles, should go between threads and never be allowed to split them. Gently pull the textile into position and then pin it to the bottom of the linen-covered hardboard in the same way. Next pin the sides. At all times be prepared to remove pins and gently pull the textile into place, adjusting until all is straight and even. It may take some time to get it quite right, taking pins out, making adjustments, easing or stretching and replacing pins but, eventually, it should be possible to get all the threads straight and the warp and weft threads of the textile at right angles to each other. Now stitch the textile on to the linen all round the edge, using linen thread and an oversewing stitch, removing the pins only after the stitches have taken over the job of keeping everything straight.

Mounting a piece in this way can be quite difficult, but it is worthwhile to go on adjusting until everything is as straight and pleasing to the eye as possible. A line in a framed piece that is wavy but should be straight can be a continuing source of irritation once the piece is framed.

Once the textile is mounted, the frame can be made to size. Choose a suitable moulding, if possible one with a deep rebate. It will be necessary to insert a very narrow fillet of wood, mitred at the corners, inside the frame so that the framed textile will never be touching the glass. A picture framer will recognise this as the way that pastels are framed. The fillet can be of natural, stained or gilded wood to suit the textile. It might even be so narrow that it cannot be seen at all. However, if it is visible, its width may be useful to cover up the stitches attaching the textile to the linen-covered hardboard mount, or its colour may serve to enhance the appearance of the textile it surrounds.

The glass itself should be sealed into the frame to prevent the entry of dust and damp and this can be done by using narrow strips of a self-adhesive masking tape (such as Tuftape, made by Copydex). Carefully applied, the sealing strip of tape is invisible from the front of the glass. When the glass has been sealed in, it should be thoroughly cleaned and dried before the fillet is inserted. (Perspex polish No. 3 is an anti-static polish and can be used on the inside of the glass). After the fillet is in position, the hardboard mount, with the textile sewn to it, should be dropped gently into position and kept in place with panel pins or brads. First put one pin in each side of the frame and then turn the frame over to check from the front that all is well and that there are no stray pieces of fluff or thread on the picture. Sometimes tapping the brads into place can cause movement, and it is as well to check before putting in all the pins. When the hardboard is in place, seal all round the edges of the back of the frame with strips of masking tape, then cover the whole back of the picture with a sheet of brown paper, sticking it to the hardboard, and finally seal round this backing with brown gummed paper to tidy the edge. Then put in screw eyes to hold the cord for hanging.

Framing lace for display can be done in much the same way although, in this case, the lace would first have to be stitched onto a backing and then the whole attached to the linen-covered hardboard in the manner described above. It pays to experiment with different-coloured backgrounds before making a final choice. Although it would seem obvious to choose a contrasting colour in order to show up the pattern of the lace, a more subtle and pleasing effect can often be achieved by choosing a backing of material only slightly darker in colour than the lace itself. Once chosen, stretch the backing onto an embroidery frame and apply

22 *A sub-frame of balsa wood and hardboard backing.*

23 *Sub-frame being covered with suitable material – adhesive on back of frame only.*

the lace to it, using as few, unobtrusive stitches as possible, only just enough to keep it in place.

An alternative to the fillet is to make a sub-frame of balsa wood and to cover this with the same material as the mount. Apply polyvinyl acetate adhesive to the back surfaces only of the sub-frame to fix on the material so that, although the other faces of the frame are covered with the material, they have no adhesive on

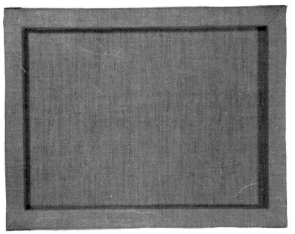

24 *Covered sub-frame and hardboard back.*

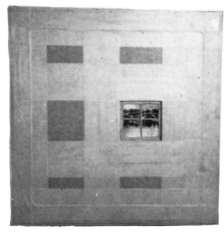

26 *Reverse side of framed Coptic weaving, showing window so that the weaving can be seen from the reverse side.*

25 *Coptic remnant framed with balsa wood sub-frame. The method of its conservation is given in Chapter 8.*

27 *Raised work (sometimes called stump work) picture in a sub-frame ready for final glazing and framing.*

them. This is the method which was used in framing the Coptic piece illustrated in **figure 25**. Remember that when using a sub-frame of this kind, the rebate of the moulding chosen for the main frame will have to be deep enough to accommodate not only the glass but also the balsa wood sub-frame and the hardboard mount. The type of moulding used in the illustration is known as hockey stick and the

frame was painted to harmonise with the background material. Of additional interest is the window cut in the hardboard backing and covered with perspex. This allows examination of the Coptic weaving from the reverse side. Stump work pictures or raised work embroidery will also need a deep sub-frame to avoid the textile coming in contact with the glass. Fans can be framed in this way, too, although specially made fan cases or box frames might be more suitable.

When cleaning the glass of either frames or display cases, choose one of two methods. Either use a damp cloth or leather, or use Perspex polish No. 3. Rubbing glass with a dry cloth can create static electricity, drawing the fibres of anything behind glass towards the glass and causing strain which, over a period of time, can cause the fibres to break, especially in the case of embroidery. A few drops of anti-static fluid (such as Comfort or Softrinse) in the water in which a duster or leather is dampened, will be an added safeguard. Perspex anti-static polish can be removed by water so, if polish-treated glass is ever washed, the polish will need to be renewed after drying.

Types of display and care

Carpets and rugs

Valuable carpets and rugs, especially those which are walked on or have furniture standing on them, should always be provided with an underfelt of natural fibres and they should be regularly vacuum-cleaned through mono-filament screening (filtration fabric). If a treasured carpet or rug requires more cleaning or needs conservation, it should be sent to a professional for treatment. There are some first-aid measures which can help to keep carpets and rugs safe and these are dealt with at the end of the chapter on tapestries. The British Museum have published a booklet about clothes moths and carpet beetles which gives valuable information and is well worth reading and keeping for reference.

Hangings

All textile hangings and curtains should be lined, both for their support and to protect them from the dust which always seems to rise and settle on the back of a hanging. In the case of curtains, a lining and interlining will give protection from some of the light they inevitably receive. If curtains are to be drawn across windows, cords should be fitted for this – they should not be pulled by hand.

The choice of lining material is important. Linings should always be lighter in weight than the textile they support; a silk embroidery would require a silk lining and an interlining of suitable material such as bump for protection and to make the piece hang well. If there is any likelihood that the lining material will shrink if it becomes damp, then it should be shrunk before use by being soaked and allowed to dry. Later shrinkage of lining can result in the lining causing damage rather than giving support to the textile.

Allow for the fact that the lining may well be stronger than the textile it is supporting, so be sure that it is attached loosely enough not to exert any drag or pull on the older and probably more fragile textile, and that it also fits well enough to give support. The linings of small hangings need only be attached round the outside edges, but larger textiles should be lined in the same way as curtains. The method of lining a large tapestry is fully described in Chapter 7 and can be adapted for lining other textiles. We would recommend the following ways of hanging a lined but unframed textile.

The piece may be suspended from a rigid pole or rod chosen for its suitability both in appearance and strength. For instance, a piece of oriental embroidery or a Tibetan tanka might look well hung from a piece of bamboo, which would be quite strong enough to take the weight, while a piece of tapestry, a rug or heavy fabric collage would require a metal rod to support it as it hangs.

A sleeve can be made at the top of the lining through which the pole is put, with the pole itself attached to the wall either by hooks at each end or by cords or chains from a central hanging point. The sleeve may be of the same material as the lining or, if the hanging is heavy, made of webbing. To make the sleeve, cut a strip of material or webbing slightly longer than the width of the hanging and make a hem at each end, if necessary, turning in the raw edges at top and bottom of the strip. Now stitch the strip in a straight line just below the top edge of the hanging. Place the hanging rod inside the strip and mark the position of the bottom edge of the

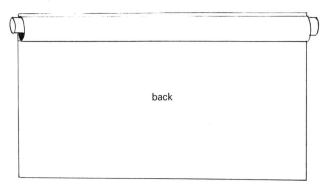

28 *Sleeve method of hanging a textile.*

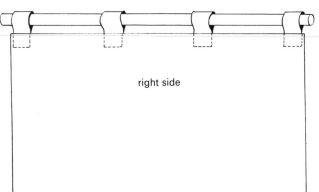

29 *Tab method of hanging a textile.*

strip on the lining, remove the rod and stitch the strip along the marked line. The little tunnel thus produced will take the rod and accommodate it in such a way that, when the textile hangs from the rod, it will hang straight down and not bulge out along the position of the rod.

A rod can also be threaded through tabs of suitable material which have been made above the top edge of the lined textile, as illustrated. This is particularly effective when hanging a textile which has been mounted onto a large piece of material, giving the appearance of a frame. The tabs would then be made of the same material as the mount. Otherwise, choose material for the tabs which complement the fabric of the hanging.

A very flimsy hanging, or one which is rather long and narrow, can be given the weight to hang down straight, provided it is evenly strong and well-supported, by inserting a rod in a sleeve at the bottom as well as at the top of the hanging. Alternatively, weight can be added to the bottom by inserting weighting strips as supplied by haberdashers for use in curtains.

The Velcro (touch-and-close fastener) method of hanging can be used successfully for small hangings as well as for tapestries, and this method is described in more detail in Chapter 7. A strip of Velcro fastener is stitched along the top edge of the lining and the corresponding strip of fastener is nailed to a batten of wood fixed to the wall where the piece is to hang. By pressing the two strips of fastener together the piece will hang safely and well-supported. Only

30 *Hanging a lined textile with Velcro (touch-and-close fastener).*

a narrow width of fastener is needed and, as in the case of its use on tapestry, the softer of the two strips is sewn to the lining while the stiffer one is nailed, with tacks, to the batten. Part of the charm and character of a textile hanging is its ability to move slightly, and one would not wish to lose this by making it too rigid. However, it is not wise to place hangings where they are constantly moved by draughts or where people can brush against them in passing, as excessive movement or rubbing will cause damage.

One way of protecting a treasured textile hanging from receiving too much light is to have another attractive, but more expendable, hanging ready to put in front of it. This is especially sensible if the room is used a lot. There are various ways to fix the protective hanging – it can be put up as a curtain and drawn aside to reveal the older textile behind it, or it could have its own hooks and merely be hung up when required as protection. Be careful that there is sufficient space between the two textiles so that the more valuable one is not rubbed when the protective hanging is drawn across or fixed in front of it.

Free-hanging textiles become dusty and should be cleaned occasionally on front and back with a vacuum cleaner through monofilament screening. The method for this is described fully in Chapter 6 on cleaning.

Textiles used in upholstery

Furniture covered with old and valuable textiles should always be placed so that they do not receive direct light and, as far as possible, in an atmosphere of constant temperature and humidity. Remember that textiles attached in any way to wood will suffer strain if the wood itself responds to changes in atmospheric conditions by contracting, expanding or warping. If furniture polish is used on the wood, be careful that none is allowed to get on to the textile upholstery as it may stain; such stains attract and hold dust and are almost impossible to remove. Silk damask, woven tapestry, embroidered canvaswork and beadwork and velvet are some of the many beautiful textiles which have been used to cover pieces of furniture. A very careful watch should be kept on such textiles, especially if there is any silk in the design of the actual material, or in the embroidery on it, as silk fibres are very vulnerable to the effects of light.

Loose covers can be used as protection, but the textiles beneath these covers need to be inspected regularly and the covers themselves kept very clean, so that particles of dust and dirt do not work their way through. Loose covers are recommended if the furniture is in use. Otherwise, if the pieces are on display and never used, some protection can be given by covering the textiles on furniture with fine net or washed silk crepeline in a suitable colour through which the design should be visible. A net or crepeline cover will not prevent actual deterioration, but it will ensure that any potentially loose threads are kept in place and not rubbed away and lost.

To fit a net or crepeline cover, smooth it gently over the textile, making sure that all its threads are in their proper place, and then secure the covering to the underneath of the seat or behind the back with stitching, using a fine, curved upholstery needle and silk thread to match the net or crepeline. If the particular design of the furniture makes it impossible to put the protective covering right over the seat or back, then fix it in place by stitching it to the edge of the textile covering, using a curved needle, silk thread and the minimum number of stitches to keep the cover in place. It may be possible to stitch it to the decorative gimp. Valuable cushion covers can be protected in a similar way.

Cleanliness is important and surface cleaning of textiles covering furniture should be done with a vacuum cleaner through monofilament screening. (See Chapter 6).

The less any old and fragile textiles are handled the better, particularly if there are any metallic threads in the design, whether in the weave or as embroidery. Apart from the unnecessary wear and tear, even apparently clean hands can be acid and cause tarnishing by touching. In professional embroidery workrooms, frequent handwashing is obligatory for those working with metal threads, and there are actually some people whose skin is so acid that,

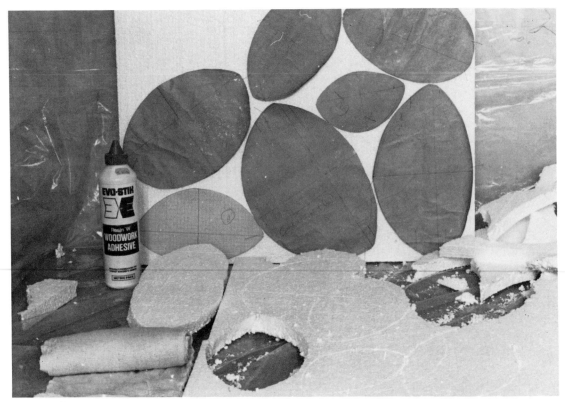

31 *Materials assembled for making a dummy.*
Background shows patterns for different layers.
Foreground shows sheet of thick polystyrene marked
for cutting, roll of stockinet for cover and adhesive on
left.

even though their hands seem clean and dry, they are unable to touch gold or silver thread without causing very rapid tarnishing. It requires an effort of will to train oneself, and tact to restrain one's friends, to resist the temptation to hold, handle and stroke precious pieces, but that restraint is a form of preventive conservation to which everyone can contribute.

Costumes
When as in silk my Julia goes,
Then, then, (methinks) how sweetly flows
That liquefaction of her clothes.
Robert Herrick, *Upon Julia's Clothes*

If old costumes are collected or owned, their continual safety will be of great importance whether they are on display or stored away to be viewed occasionally and, if one cares for them responsibly, they should never be worn or even tried on. The exceptions here are wedding veils and christening robes, when sentimental or traditional reasons for their being worn might outweigh all other considerations; we deal with these items in more detail later.

If a costume is to be put on display at any time, it should be supported in such a way that no strain is imposed on any part of the fabric. Ideally, one would use dummies made to the exact measurements for each separate costume and would dress the dummies first in the proper undergarments, making especially sure that such intrinsic parts of the costume as, for instance, a bustle, are used under the displayed costume, rather than trying to achieve an effect with padding only. Proper underclothing, even petticoats, beneath a costume, not only give the correct appearance but also act as support for the textile of the garment.

A method of making dummies to exact mea-

32 *The pieces assembled by glueing – front view.*

34 *Shaping the dummy with padding.*

33 *Side view of dummy after assembly of polystyrene pieces.*

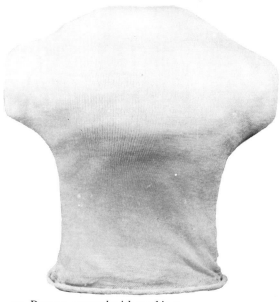

35 *Dummy covered with stockinet.*

surements is illustrated here, using thick, oval pieces of polystyrene cut out and built up, one above another, and glued together until the shape and size from shoulders to waist is roughly what is required. Once the glue is dry

and the piece assembled, the exact measurements can be achieved by sculpting the polystyrene. The whole piece is then covered with stockinet and any further shaping added with padding under the stockinet wherever this is

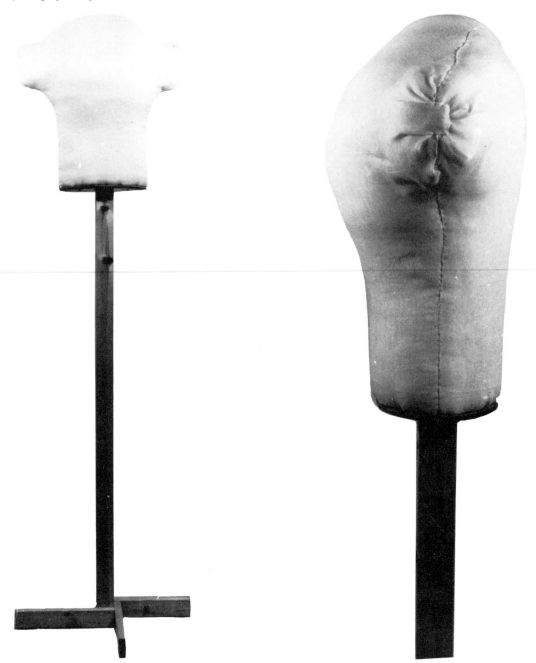

36 *Dummy on stand – front view.*   **37** *Closer look at dummy on stand from side.*

38 *Specially constructed dummy for eighteenth-century riding habit.*

needed. Crumpled acid-free tissue paper can be used as padding to fill out the costume in such areas as the sleeves. Costumes are always more safely displayed in the round on a dummy than by using any method which would involve pinning to keep the garment in a display position, say on a board that is either sloping or vertical, as this causes strain from the points of contact and can, in quite a short time, result in considerable damage.

Any creases in a silk or woollen garment will fall out and disappear if the costume is put on to a dummy or hung up on a well-padded hanger. Ironing should be avoided if at all possible and certainly no textile should be ironed, even at the low temperature (100°C, 212°F) we would allow, unless it has been cleaned. The heat of an iron can set any stains permanently and any acid

dust on the textile could be sealed into the fabric by the application of heat. If a costume is to be shown for any length of time, it should be housed in a display case with a cool, dry atmosphere inside, sealed against the entry of dust and damp and exposed to a minimum of light, with an arrangement for complete light exclusion at times when the costume is not actually being viewed. Silica gel crystals in the case will be some protection against damp, but the effectiveness of these crystals is limited and they have to be watched carefully so as to be dried out when they have become saturated. These crystals are deep blue in colour when completely dry, but change colour gradually to light pink as they absorb moisture. When they reach this pale pink colour, they should be removed and dried out in mild heat until they resume their original deep blue colour.

This cycle of regeneration can be repeated several times before the crystals need to be replaced with fresh ones. Unused crystals can be safely stored in an airtight container.

The temptation to wear and display old and beautiful clothes is great and it can certainly be argued that, as clothes are made to be worn, it is only when they are on living and moving people that they can really be appreciated. This argument has validity, but against it can be set the facts that any handling is potentially damaging to an old textile and that great stress and strain is imposed on a costume by dressing and undressing, especially if the wearer is not quite the right size for the garment and is not wearing the underclothing appropriate for the period of the costume. Wearing can also result in staining from perspiration or spilled food and drink. Sitting down in a fragile dress could well ruin it for ever. It would be worthwhile for a collector determined to display costumes on living models to have copies made for wearing, in order that the originals may be kept safe.

There is another way of showing a costume collection safely, again and again, and that is by making a film or video recording. People of the right sizes, wearing underclothing appropriate to the costumes, their hair styled correctly and carrying the right accessories, could model the

clothes in suitable settings and all could be recorded. Obviously a good deal of planning would have to be done and an undertaking of this kind would be expensive, but an added interest would be created if details of the cut, material and stitching of the different costumes were to be shown in close-up. The finished film would be both interesting and educational, much more revealing than a series of photographs and much less dangerous to the costumes than constant wearing and handling.

39 *A riding habit of the first half of the eighteenth century made from a material combining silk and wool, before conservation. The deterioration of the silk is very obvious.*

40 *After conservation the riding habit is displayed on its specially made dummy. The costume was not taken apart for treatment but, supported on the dummy, the material was conserved by being couched onto supporting silk crepeline to secure the degraded silk fibres and strengthen the whole fabric. (The riding habit belongs to Saffron Walden Museum).*

5

Storage

The greatest number of textiles which have survived from very early times are those which have been discovered in tombs, particularly in Egypt and South America. They could well have been new and of good quality when they were sealed away in what were virtually ideal conditions for the safe keeping of textiles – cool, dry and dark surroundings, with a constant temperature and humidity, unpolluted air and, of course, no handling or disturbance.

Their state of preservation provides a good lesson in the safe keeping of stored textiles. The opposite is true of airing cupboards, which seem to be unique to Britain. Certainly those airing cupboards built around unlagged hot water storage tanks have been responsible for damage found in weakened and discoloured fibres along folds and creases, due to pressure, overheating and high humidity. Fortunately, an airing cupboard is not normally considered as storage for treasured textiles, although it is not unknown for some quite old and valued table or bed linen, not in constant use, to be put there and forgotten until it is too late to prevent damage. The provision of a suitable storage environment is one which must, of course, depend on the facilities available.

Safe storage

Few people, if any, can hope to provide anything approaching the equable climatic conditions afforded by a burial chamber! However, everyone trying to supply safe storage for their textiles can do their best in existing or achievable circumstances, using cupboards, shelving to hold boxes, chests of drawers or even special rooms, according to the size and number of the textiles to be stored. The aim should be to provide space that will be dark and dry with a cool, even temperature, clean air and sufficient room to accommodate the textiles without overcrowding.

The textiles, when stored, should be as clean as possible so that dust and dirt, the acids of atmospheric pollution or the presence of moths or other pests will not cause unavoidable deterioration during storage. (The method of cleaning textiles is a subject in itself and this is dealt with later). A stored textile should not be subjected to any strain or movement which can cause the fibres to become weak and break. Strain can be avoided by seeing that the textiles are supported during storage and are not pressed into sharp folds which will weaken the fibres bent under pressure.

A really good supply of acid-free tissue paper will be needed to protect the textiles. This tissue paper is sold in packets or larger quantities (see the list of suppliers at the back of the book). Small, flat textiles, for example pieces of lace or similar items, can be stored lying smooth and unfolded, with plenty of acid-free tissue paper above and below each piece. Provided that the pieces are not heavy and are quite flat, they can lie on top of each other. Always keep a reference of the position of each item – either with a list on top showing the order or by tabs between each

41 *Lengths of lace stored, rolled round tissue-covered cylinders, in a tissue-lined box, each tagged for identification.*

layer – to make identification simple and so that each piece is readily accessible without unduly disturbing the other objects. Never use self-adhesive tape nor allow any other adhesive in the form of labels to come into contact with the textiles.

Larger flat pieces which have one side short enough to fit on to a storage shelf or into a drawer and small, long pieces, such as ribbons, narrow pieces of lace or strips of embroidery, should be stored rolled, but not too tightly, around a cylinder of some sort, again using plenty of acid-free tissue paper so that the textile is protected on each side. The cardboard cylinders from toilet or kitchen paper rolls are useful for narrow pieces. Be sure to cover the cylinder with several layers of tissue paper before rolling the textile onto it as some cardboard contains acids harmful to textiles. It is wise to assume

that all cardboard can harm textiles and to protect them from it with several layers of tissue paper in all circumstances.

If a textile can be rolled, this should be done with the right side of the piece facing outermost; this is especially important if the textile is lined so that the right side of the piece will remain smooth even if the lining becomes creased through the difference in tension caused by rolling the piece round the cylinder. It may seem odd to roll an embroidered piece right side outermost, but it is correct and best for the textile. The right side should, of course, be covered with tissue paper as the rolling proceeds.

For larger flat textiles, a length of polythene drainpipe, well covered with tissue paper, makes a good cylinder as it is very light in weight and about the right circumference. Larger cylinders made of cardboard can be obtained from shops selling dress materials or carpets. The pieces, once rolled, can be stored in the dark, either on shelves, in drawers or in boxes – again

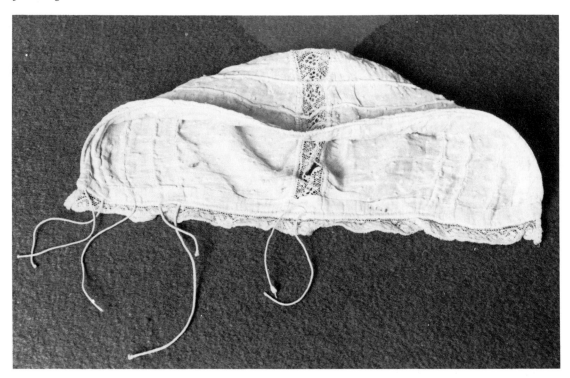

42 *Baby's bonnet before conservation.*

all lined with acid-free tissue paper. Always store cylinders lying down and supported along their length. Cylinders should never be stored standing on end, no matter how space-saving an idea this may seem as, by reducing the support, the rolled textile might also become damaged through sliding downwards on the cylinder.

Really large objects, and anything shaped or lined, may have to be folded to fit the storage space available. Any folds necessary should be made very loosely over quite thick rolls of acid-free tissue paper. If the textile is pressed down to give a fold with a sharp edge, the fibres along that fold will be weakened and will eventually break. Stored textiles that have had to be folded should be opened out occasionally and refolded in different places. Particular care should be taken that any pleats in stored costumes have rolls of tissue paper under them, supporting them, so that the strain on the fibres along the pleat edge is relieved as much as possible. Again, a tag on the outside to identify each piece will save time in finding it and prevent unnecessary disturbance of other pieces.

Costumes

The storing of costumes presents quite complicated problems, often requiring individual solutions. Small items can be stored flat. Bonnets and other small, shaped pieces should be filled with crumpled acid-free tissue paper until they assume their correct shapes and then put onto shelves or in boxes but, of course, never one piece on top of another. Garments may be stored on dummies of the right size and shape, and covered with washed calico or gingham bags, closed at the tops to prevent any dust settling on the garment, but left open at the bottom to allow the air to circulate. The bag must be large enough not to crush the garment in any way. The use of plastic or polythene bags in storage is not recommended. When new a polythene bag can hold humidity, and if anything placed in it is not perfectly clean and dry the bag will provide ideal conditions for the growth of mildew or similar moulds. Polythene seems to attract dust which lies on its surface and, unfortunately, as it gets older, it seems to develop tiny holes through which the dust goes on to the surface of whatever is being covered. Cellophane is a safer cover but has the distinct disadvantage of tearing very easily and, therefore, a fabric cover would seem to be the safest and most durable to use.

Ideally, each costume should be stored on its own dummy made to its proportions. Dressing a dummy for storage is exactly the same as dressing it for display, putting on first the underwear, including bustle, underbodice, etc., as required and using original garments or copies. However, in storage it is wise to use a great deal of acid-free tissue paper, as mentioned already, to achieve fullness and shape so that there will be as few folds and creases in the stored garment as possible, and so that maximum support will be given to the material. Quite a lot of tissue paper will be required, even on a specially-made dummy, particularly in the sleeves, bodice and around the hips. When storing a costume, stitch several tapes to the

43 *Baby's bonnet after conservation and prepared for safe storage. Crumpled tissue paper, and some net for extra firmness, gives proper shape, held in place by soft cotton material.*

44 *A collection of baby clothes in storage in a deep tissue-lined box. A chart on the box lid will identify the position of each item for easy retrieval.*

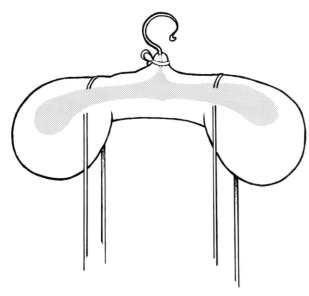

45 *Padded hanger with tapes to attach to skirt top to relieve strain on top section of costume while hanging.*

46 *Incorrectly hung costume.*

inside of the top of the skirt and then pin the other ends of the tapes to the dummy or padded hanger, using brass lacepins or safety pins. By making the tapes just short enough, it is possible to let them take some of the weight of the skirt and this will greatly lessen the strain on the fabric of the bodice.

If dummies are not available, costumes can be stored on hangers, very well padded with cotton wool, and the costume then covered with washed calico or gingham. Never allow a costume to hang from an ordinary unpadded hanger. The photograph illustrates only too clearly what can happen. As with costumes on dummies, a very great deal of tissue paper will be needed in the sleeves, bodices and upper parts of the skirts of costumes stored on hangers. Try to make costumes assume, as nearly as possible, their intended shape, eliminating unwanted folds and creases. Tapes again, from the inside tops of the skirts to the hangers, will help to take the strain of the weight of the skirts from the material of the bodices. Calico bags,

open at the bottom and closed at the top, should cover the costumes in storage. It is very important to make sure that costumes on hangers are also not packed too closely together, as could well happen if the hangers are put on to a rail in a cupboard. Pushing the costumes together can result in creasing and folding. Here again, we come to the question of space. Tie a label on the top of each calico bag for easy identification of the garment in it.

Storing a number of costumes on dummies will take up a great deal of space, as the dummies should not be so near together that the garments get crushed. If an open room, rather than a cupboard, is selected as a store, then be sure that the light is excluded and that the temperature and humidity are constant and suitable.

The other method of storing costumes is to lay them flat in large boxes, drawers or on shelving. This would be the only sensible way to store a heavily embroidered costume or one with beading on a fragile material, as can be found in some of the dresses from the turn of the century. In such costumes, the weight of the decoration could easily cause damage unless the material of the garment is adequately supported. A dress made of material cut on the cross should always be stored lying flat or it will drop out of shape. Again, a great deal of acid-free tissue paper is needed, with layers below and above each garment and crumpled into sleeves and bodices, so that all folds and creases are eliminated as far as possible and the fabric can rest easily and is well supported. If cardboard boxes are used to store costumes, first line the boxes with several layers of acid-free tissue paper. If costumes are stored in drawers or on shelving, place a dust sheet lightly over the top of them for added protection and avoid, if at all possible, putting costumes one above another in boxes, drawers or on shelves. If this method of storage is unavoidable, try to work out an order so that they can exert the least possible pressure on each other.

Always make sure that anything hard, sharp or rough on the surface of a stored textile, whether it is in the form of a fastening, embroidery, beads or other decoration, has sufficient padding or protection covering it in storage so that it cannot harm any other textile with which it may come into contact.

Smaller items

Fans

Fans in poor condition which are stored should be loosely open so that there is the least possible strain. Apart from the tissue paper above and below each fan, make up the difference in height between the guards at each side of the fan with rolls of tissue paper to give the fan complete support, and let it lie as flat as possible.

Gloves

Gloves may be stored with folded tissue paper in the fingers and cuffs to suggest their proper shape, and to relax old creases and prevent new ones forming.

Parasols

The storing of parasols presents a problem. Fully open, the material of the cover is stretched, which causes strain, yet if a parasol is stored closed and rolled the material is again subject to strain from tight folding. If there is sufficient storage room, the covers suffer the least strain if the parasol can be kept just slightly open. Rolls of tissue paper in the loose folds of the cover will ease the material so that the fibres cannot be pressed into sharp folds. Parasols, loosely open, can be supported upright by attaching their handles to a rod across a cupboard, their ferrules just touching the floor, provided they are not allowed to crush or brush against each other. In a later chapter we describe the conservation of a very pretty Victorian parasol and the method evolved to take the strain of tension on the cover of an open parasol by stitching a tape round the inside edge of the cover.

Dolls

Dolls are best stored individually in boxes, lined with acid-free tissue paper. Lay the doll on a piece of strong clean material which is as long as, and about three times the width of, the doll.

47 *Large size tray/frame of module system for collection of Peruvian pieces which the owner wished to use as illustrations when lecturing. The collection should, therefore, be capable of being easily and safely transported.*

Insert rolls of tissue paper under all the potential folds in the doll's clothes to make sure that the material cannot be pressed down into sharp-edged folds. Place a piece of tissue over the whole doll and lift it into the box by holding the sides of the material on which the doll lies. Then fold the side pieces of material across the front of the doll. Removal of the doll for examination is then easy, as it can be lifted out of the box without being handled at all. This method of storage can be adapted for a number of shaped or very fragile objects.

Very deep lightweight frames with fabric bottoms, like the one used for framing the Coptic fragment, can be stacked on top of each other, each one containing some fragile part of a collection. These could even be stored in nicely made containers and lifted out for viewing by means of tapes or tabs.

Examine all textiles, especially stored ones, regularly but carefully. The use of any preparation to kill or deter moths or other insect pests may also have harmful effects on textiles themselves, and possibly humans too if used in confined spaces. We believe that cleanliness and constant vigilance is the surest moth-proofing there is, provided handling is kept to a minimum. A regular safety check can, however, be

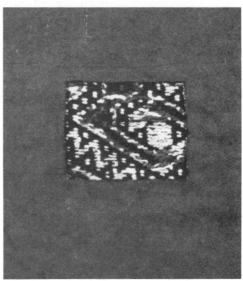

48 *Window in backing of textile in Figure 47 so that reverse side of weaving may be studied.*

OPPOSITE ABOVE
49 *Two half-sized tray frames. Small textiles are attached at one end to the backing with a hinge of fabric while attached at the other end with Velcro. Thus the Peruvian piece can be lifted, by undoing the Velcro, so that the reverse can be examined, but the piece cannot be entirely removed from the frame.*

OPPOSITE
50 *The frames are made on a module system so that they fit together stacked according to size.*

the time to vary the folding pattern in large stored textiles, and should always be done as standard practice when displays are altered.

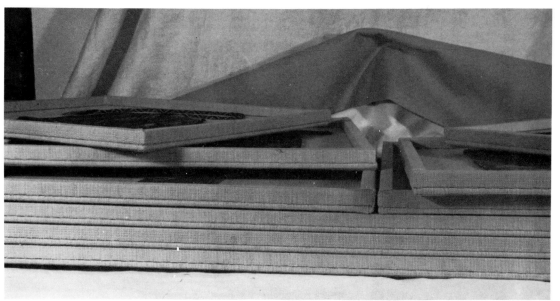

51 *The frames are placed on their specially-made casing and secured by tapes.*

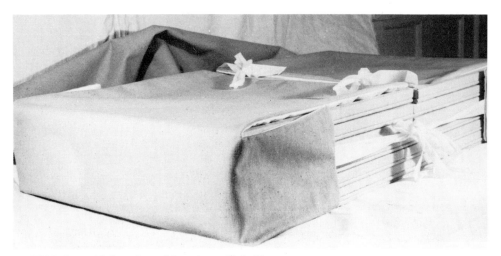

52 *With the padded top in position, the padded sides and top of the carrying case fold round the frames and are then secured.*

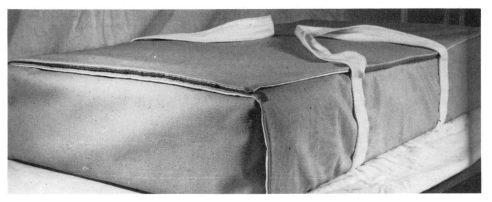

53 *With its padded casing and tape handles for carrying, the transportation of the collection for display or illustration of lectures is both easy and safe.*

6

Cleaning

She did not recognise her enemy,
She thought him Dust,
But what is Dust, save Time's most lethal weapon,
Her faithful ally and our sneaking foe?
Sir Osbert Sitwell, *Mrs Southern's Diary*

All textiles should be kept as clean as possible, whether on display or in storage, and, in particular, a textile should be clean before it receives any further treatment of conservation or restoration.

Surface cleaning

Vacuum cleaning, to remove dust, is the easiest form of cleaning for the operator and the least hazardous for the textile, and regular careful surface cleaning is recommended for all textiles on display in open conditions. Hanging textiles need to be cleaned only occasionally, but textiles presenting horizontal surfaces on which dust can collect – for instance carpets and the uphol-stery on furniture – require more frequent cleaning. The easiest method of cleaning the surface of a textile is to cover it with monofilament screening over which the hand-held nozzle of the dusting attachment of a vacuum cleaner can be moved quite safely to collect the dust. This screening, also known as filtration fabric, has a very smooth mesh and is reasonably rigid. It is heavy enough to be laid firmly on the textile so that neither the fabric itself or its fibres are sucked up by the vacuum, while the dust is drawn through the mesh into

54 *Vacuum cleaning through monofilament screening (filtration fabric).*

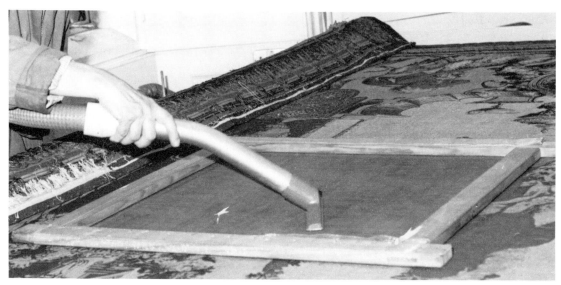

the nozzle of the cleaner. This screening is sold by length and is about 36 in (90 cm) wide. (For stockists see the list of suppliers.) For surface cleaning, a piece measuring about 36 in (90 cm) square is adequate as this can be moved around over the whole surface of the textile until it has all been cleaned. As the monofilament screening frays very easily when cut and the raw edges are sharp, it is wise to bind the edges with tape or thin webbing. The screening is also very useful as a support for textiles during washing, so it is worthwhile indicating separate pieces used for different reasons by using different coloured bindings – say white for screening used in washing and red used in vacuum cleaning – and to remember to keep clean the pieces used with the vacuum cleaner by washing them, separately, from time to time. The screening can also be framed with thin, smooth slats of wood to make a more rigid and easily moved permanent cleaning accessory. If no screening is available, it is possible to surface-clean a textile by tying a piece of fine net over the hand-held nozzle of the dusting attachment of a vacuum cleaner and moving this over *and a little above* the textile. This method is not really recommended except in emergencies, as great care must be taken that the nozzle does not touch the surface of the textile being cleaned; this could so easily cause damage, especially if any part of the textile came in contact with the cleaner or loose threads were drawn up by the suction. The use of monofilament screening makes surface cleaning safer for the textile and easier and quicker for the operator.

Brushing, however carefully done, may cause damage and is inefficient in that it tends to move dust around rather than remove it. In the cleaning of raised work, dust which has collected in crevices can be gently brushed out with a sable paint brush so that it can be removed later by the vacuum through screening.

The use of spot cleaners on any textile *in situ* is not recommended, and neither is surface cleaning with a liquid. Any liquid, even plain water, can combine with the chemical content of dust, dirt and the acids of air pollution, with damaging effects which may not be immediately

apparent but which cannot be rectified afterwards. The cleaning of upholstery while still on furniture, other than the removal of surface dust, should not be attempted.

Any form of chemical dry-cleaning in enclosed premises can be dangerous, not only for the textile but for the operator too, and should not be attempted. There are specialist dry-cleaning firms which will undertake careful cleaning, giving individual attention to special orders, and such firms can be approached to clean dirty but obviously strong textile pieces. It is as well to remember that the decision to have the piece cleaned must ultimately be that of the owner or the person responsible for the care of the textile, and no dry-cleaning firm will accept responsibility for the decision to have the work done. The fluids used in dry-cleaning can cause reactions with the fibres and finishes of some old textiles and this may have unfortunate results. Therefore, if the piece is either historically or artistically important, it should be taken to an expert textile conservator for cleaning.

If, however, a piece is not of national importance and, though dirty, is obviously strong, as might be the case with curtains or an item of costume, then dry-cleaning could be done by the person in charge of it in one of the coin-operated do-it-yourself machines with a short cleaning cycle, preferably just after the cleaning fluid has been renewed. To prepare the textile for cleaning, first detach anything from it – such as rings or hooks on a curtain – which would be likely to snag or catch any part of the fabric. If a garment is to be cleaned, remove any buttons with no textile content – metal or horn, for instance. Secure all hooks, eyes and other fastenings and tack a piece of strong net or a ribbon over both the front and back of any fastenings so that they cannot come undone and cause any damage during cleaning.

If there are any other parts of the garment which might be fragile, tack pieces of net over those areas. Make the net patch very much larger than the suspect frail area and take long tacking stitches into the stronger surrounding fabric, using silk thread, a fine needle and fairly loose stitches so that nothing can drag or pull.

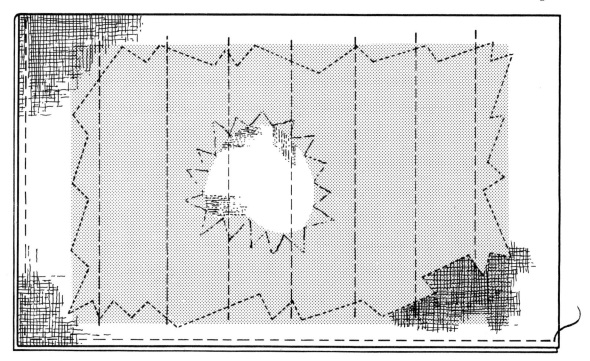

55 *Fragile textile prepared for cleaning.*

Also make several rows of long tacking stitches in each direction across the frail area to attach the net and make sure that it will really give support. Again, tension is important – stitches should give firmness without being too tight. Now put the prepared textile into a bag made from an old nylon net curtain and sew it up all round before taking it to the dry cleaners.

All this takes time and needs care and may seem excessive pampering of a textile already defined as strong, but prevention of damage is always essential because a complete repair of damage is never possible. After cleaning hang the textile, on a padded hanger if it is a garment, out in the fresh air to help any creases fall out and to allow all the fumes from the dry-cleaning fluid to disappear.

Washing

With many textiles, however, the question arises whether the most effective way of cleaning would be to wash the piece. An experienced conservator, aware of the ethics of conservation which recommend that only methods of treatment which are reversible should be used – that is to say, that anything that is done can be undone – knows that washing is an irreversible and potentially dangerous process and can be justified only if the end result will be the safe removal of harmful soiling matter which, if retained, would contribue to increasing deterioration. Any decision to wash a textile is one which should not be made without a great deal of thought, research and tests. Every decision must be a separate one, relating to one particular object. Experience will obviously be a guide in a decision but nothing should ever be taken for granted. This is an attitude which it may be difficult for some of us to cultivate, since the making, washing and repairing of household linen and clothing is something which, throughout history, has been part of domestic life, but it does not follow that everyone has been equally skilled in these tasks. Individuals have obviously possessed a greater or lesser degree of competency and when the occasional failure occurred – a colour running in the wash or something that should never have been washed disintegrating

56 *Regimental colour of the Royal Sussex Regiment dated prior to 1801. The shape and colour of the flag was reproduced and pieces of the silk remnants placed in their original positions. Such time-consuming conservation is important when dealing with an historic textile.*

in the process – it was seldom an irretrievable disaster. Clothes and household linens normally wear out and require replacement anyway, and an accident or misjudgement could be regarded as merely hastening the inevitable. Successful washing techniques have always needed care, a fact recognised by the many recipes for the safe washing of textiles in books of household management from very early dates. Since the introduction of the more complex man-made fibres which are not always easy to identify, today's fabrics are usually labelled with specific instructions for washing. Some manufacturers, however, still rely on traditional experience by stating simply 'wash as wool'. In the event of a washing failure of a modern fabric, a manufacturer would almost certainly put the blame on the operator for not following the instructions, however vague.

Washing an old textile, however, is a very different matter and there can never be any standard directions. So, first of all, there is the problem of identifying the fibre or fibres of the textile, the method of manufacture, the dyes and finishes which have been used and the composition of whatever has made the textile dirty and soiled, including the dust hidden by linings and, sometimes, several interlinings. Secondly, one must assess the condition of the textile, taking into account that all old fibres are almost certainly fragile and that some fibres, even when new and strong, are more vulnerable to damage when they are wet and can more easily tear and break when heavy with water. Finally, one must assess the condition and composition of any old repairs, decide if their colours would be fast to washing and, if so, whether to remove them before or after washing. If there is no likelihood of the colour running, old repairs can be some support during the washing process and the decision about whether or not to remove them for aesthetic reasons can be made when the object is clean.

Few textiles with a painted design can be washed. This applies to flags and banners, too, but a fragile banner which has been exposed to atmospheric pollution, whether it has a painted design or not, would have become so acid that putting it into water could be to create a virtual acid bath and result in the disintegration of the textile into a sort of banner soup. The conservation of old flags and banners is professional work. Silk which has been given any form of dressing during its manufacture might never look or feel the same after washing and, therefore, no treated silk should be washed. This would apply to most silk garments.

Loose dyes

Some dyes can run or bleed if allowed to become wet. Testing by applying wet cotton wool to an unobtrusive corner of the fabric or embroidery will help to establish if the dyes are relatively fast, but always be wary and careful. The dyes in nineteenth- and early twentieth-century materials, including those used for embroidery silks, are very liable to run. If the dyes appear to be

57 *The dark staining is due to previous washing with lining in place.*

fast but you have some reservations, perhaps because of the date of the object, make sure you hasten the drying process after washing by the use of blotting paper or other absorbent material.

If the object to be washed is lined, then the lining and any interlining should be removed and the washing of lining and textile treated as two separate and entirely different problems. The photograph shows what can happen if a lined piece is washed with the lining still in place. The dust and dirt trapped between lining and textile have set up chemical reactions permanently marking the textile. The piece was brought for treatment and, unfortunately, even taking it all apart and rewashing the two textiles separately did not remove the marks, yet it is possible that after the very first washing and rinsing all seemed to have been successfully cleaned.

This illustrates an important point. It is quite wrong to assume that washing, however carefully done, will necessarily remove all the dust, dirt and pollution. Not only is it necessary to have the right equipment, use the right washing agents and water, but of very great importance is the technique of rinsing which, unless understood and faithfully followed, can result in the redeposition of the soiling matter in such a way that it can never be removed.

The importance of rinsing

Washing agents recommended for conservation as being the most suitable for the washing of old textiles are very effective in lifting soiled matter from the textile fibres during washing, but not so good at holding these matters in suspension. Consequently, having been lifted off the fibres, the particles of dust and dirt may fall back onto the textile and then become very difficult to move. Repeated washings will, unfortunately, not remove them, but result in a build-up of immovable soiling. However, by constantly rinsing away the dirty water during the washing process, the opportunity for the soiling matter, initially released into the water by the action of the washing agent, to fall back again on the textile is much less likely to be presented. Changing the water in the washing bath as often as is possible, and certainly before it becomes really dirty, can mean that the least possible amount of soil is deposited back onto the textile.

The importance of softened water

Constant rinsing means using a great deal of water, and that means softened water when washing important textiles. The presence of calcium, magnesium and iron salts in normal tap water remains a major factor even in soft-water areas. The only way to try to overcome the soil redistribution when washing any precious textile is to use water which has been through a proprietary household water softener (such as Permutit) or a de-ioniser. This applies to *all* the water used during the washing processes. Make

sure that the washing water is constantly drained away as it becomes dirty and that rinsing continues for as long as possible, certainly until the water is clear. If water from neither a softener nor a de-ioniser is available, a supply of softened water must be prepared in receptacles by treating tap water with a preparation such as Calgon according to the instructions on the packet, for use in washing and early rinsing, but be sure to use de-ionised or distilled water for the final rinse. De-ionised water can be bought in household stores in bottles for use in steam irons and distilled water from a chemist. Do not use distilled water sometimes available at garages for topping up batteries.

Preparations

Home, and being washing day, dined upon cold meat.

Samuel Pepys, *Diary*

If a considered decision to wash a textile is taken, then every step of the washing process should be carried out with thought and care. All textiles should be washed lying flat and supported, and handling should be kept to the absolute minimum. If the textile is reasonably strong, then laying it flat on a piece of monofilament screening, by which it can be lowered into and

58 *A Coptic remnant supported on screening for washing.*

59 *Makeshift washing tank.*

raised from the washing vessel, will be protection enough. If the piece is delicate, sandwich it between two layers of the screening and tack the layers together around the outside so that the textile cannot move around during washing. If the piece is very fragile, protect the fibres with net in the way described for preparing a piece for dry cleaning, and then sandwich the textile between two pieces of screening. Try to see that the whole textile is supported and that there is the least possible chance of the fragile fibres being broken, twisted or pulled out of shape during washing and drying.

Textiles used in upholstery
The textiles to be washed may be covers from pieces of furniture, such as stool tops, chair or sofa seats, backs and armpieces. When a fabric is removed from a piece of furniture for washing, this should be done with great care, not only so that there is no avoidable damage to the old textile covering, but also because the original upholstery materials and methods have their own historical interest, and what is found should be recorded in notes and sketches as the pieces are removed. It is always desirable to aim

at replacing anything that is in good enough condition, such as the studs which hold the fabric to the wood and the gimp, if it can be cleaned, and any necessary repairs effected. On the other hand, of course, this could well be the right time to renew webbing and do any re-upholstery that may have become desirable. If replacements are necessary, try to preserve examples of the original materials to be kept with the documentation on the piece, so that all knowledge of the original upholstery materials and methods are not lost. As each textile piece is very carefully removed from the furniture, mark it with a few strands of coloured cotton – a different colour for each piece. Keep a record of where the pieces came from and of the colours marking them. Next make a template, in paper, of each piece, also marking this with the same colour. There should then be no doubt about the size, shape and the exact position on the furniture to which each piece of upholstery material belongs. Prepare for cleaning by supporting fragile areas with screening or net and then, before washing, surface clean each piece on both sides, using a vacuum cleaner and screening, to remove as much loose dust and dirt as possible.

Equipment

Now assemble the equipment needed for washing. The first requirement will be a flat-bottomed vessel large enough to allow the textile to lie completely flat. If you are washing a small item there is seldom a problem in finding a suitable washing vessel, as the kitchen sink, a bowl or bath will do. Especially useful are the shallow developing tanks used by photographers. If the piece to be washed is much larger than can be accommodated in an existing vessel, it is possible to rig up a washing tank on a terrace or lawn. Choose an area with a smooth surface but, even so, pad the proposed site with a really thick layer of cardboard and newspaper to eliminate the risk of an uneven surface of bumps, hollows or sharp ridges which might not be apparent to the eye but which could cause some damage to the textile when pressed down onto the floor of the tank during the washing process. Outline the four sides of the tank, using bricks (two layers should give a reasonable depth) or wooden beams, making sure that there will be room enough inside the area for the textile to lie quite flat. To make the tank, cover the whole outlined bath with a sheet of heavy duty polythene sheeting, making sure it fits the bottom and goes over the sides, and anchor it down with a few bricks or stones round the outside edge as illustrated.

A copious supply of *softened* water, preferably at a temperature of about 30°C (86°F) – which feels just warm to the hands – will be needed for washing and rinsing, with distilled or de-ionised water for the final rinse.

The water we use for our washing has been through a Permutit water softener which treats the calcium and other minerals in the water passing through it; the appliance needs regular replenishment with common salt. We also have a de-ioniser which produces purer water.

If tap water has to be used, even in soft-water districts, for washing and initial rinsing, it should first be softened in jugs or other containers by adding Calgon or some other proprietary water softener in proportions recommended by the manufacturers. Distilled or de-ionised water should always be used for the final rinse.

Synperonic NDB (formerly known as Lissapol), Vulpex and Saponaria are all suitable washing agents (see list of suppliers). Synperonic should be used in a one per cent solution, adding two 5 ml medicine spoonfuls of Synperonic liquid to 1¾ pt (1 l) of water. Vulpex may be used in a five per cent solution – ten 5 ml spoonfuls to 1¾ pt (1 l) of water – and Saponaria is bought in packets which have instructions on them for preparation. If only a small amount of washing is to be done with Saponaria at any one time, it is wise to make up only a small quantity as it does not keep well.

All these washing agents are mild in action and suitable for washing delicate textiles, while almost all the usual washing powders, soaps and detergents on the market contain chemicals and optical bleaches which may make the normal weekly wash whiter than white but which might cause undesirable changes in an old textile; they should not, therefore, be used in conservation.

A soft flat sponge will be needed for the actual washing; a synthetic sponge is quite suitable. A piece of softboard is useful, and sometimes necessary, so that washed textiles can be pinned out to dry but, as softboard contains acid, it should always be covered with a sheet of melinex or polythene.

The washing process

First make quite sure that everything that will be needed is to hand and prepared and that the textile is supported adequately and safely. It is recommended that washing is done in warm water, but the rinsing processes can be done in cold water if that is more convenient.

So, having put some warm softened water mixed with a little of the diluted washing agent into the washing vessel, carefully lower the supported textile into the water and allow it to become properly saturated. Next press the sponge gently onto the textile to move the suds and water through it to release the soiling matter. Never rub or squeeze an old textile, only press the sponge onto it, moving the sponge along after each press by lifting it out of the water so that eventually the whole of the textile has had suds and water pressed through it. At this point it is wise to rinse away the first washing water, and with it any dirt already released, before repeating the washing process. Continue in this fashion until the washing water appears clean, and so does the water from the next rinse. Continue rinsing until all suds have gone and then give the final rinse in distilled or de-ionised water. If washing is being done in an improvised tank outside, water can be drained from the tank during the repeated changes of water advocated by removing the support at one corner to allow drainage from the tank, not forgetting, of course, to rebuild the tank before putting more water in.

It is important, in all washing, not to allow the textile to remain in dirty water even for a short time, for the reasons already mentioned. Therefore over- (rather than under-) rinse and be sure that the final rinsing is done with the purest possible water.

The clean textile should be dried flat, right side uppermost, smoothed into shape or, in the case of lace or materials for which templates were made, pinned out into position on a piece of softboard which has been covered with melinex film, polythene or blotting paper. The pins used should be brass lace pins as softboard is acid and any other pins can be affected by this.

60 *Successive samples of drainage water from rinsing during the washing process.*

61 *Lace pinned out to dry on melinex-covered softboard.*

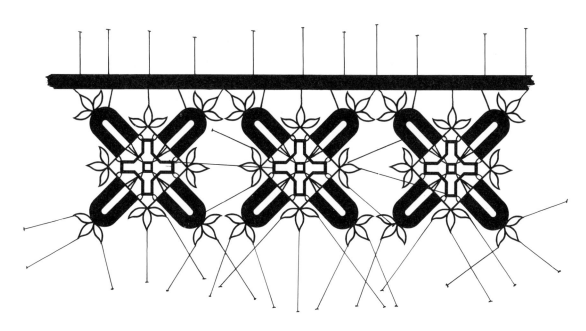

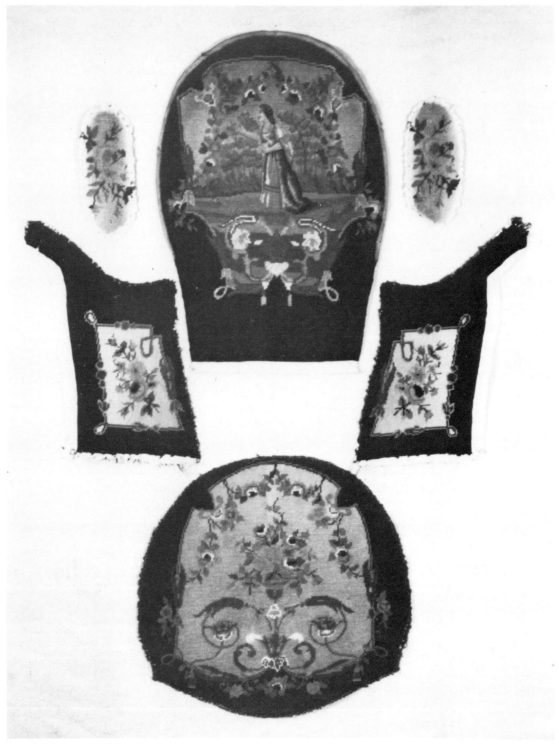

62 *Canvas-work covers from upholstered chair drying in shape having been pinned out in shape on their templates.*

All pieces should be allowed to dry naturally away from bright light, especially sunlight and artificial heat. If there is any suspicion that the colours may run, the drying process may be hastened by the careful use of blotting paper or clean towels. Large pieces, such as a woven tapestry or canvas-work furniture covers which have been washed in an improvised washing tank outside, should not be left to dry there, even if the day is not especially sunny, but should be blotted with absorbent material to remove some of the water, rolled with more absorbent material round a cylinder, and transported indoors on the cylinder supported by two people, to be unrolled and laid to dry flat, right-side uppermost. It will be found that even the largest objects take a surprisingly short time to dry by this method, generally overnight.

Canvas-work and tapestry furniture covers should be pinned out, right side uppermost, on melinex-covered softboard or on a floor covered with polythene, using the templates to get them to dry into their proper shape and size, with the warp and weft threads aligned at right angles to each other. Such pieces can be very gently pulled into shape when they are wet and the pinning altered until this is so.

Christening robes

A cotton christening robe should always be washed before storing, especially if the garment has been starched, as starch left in a stored textile can cause damage to the fibres and provide food for pests.

After washing flat, supported on monofilament screening exactly as described for other textiles, the robe can be dried by being rolled first in a clean white towel to remove some of the water and then hung on a small padded hanger and allowed to dry naturally. It should be gently smoothed and pulled into shape as it dries. When quite dry, it can be stored, using plenty of acid-free tissue paper crumpled into the sleeves and upper part – which may well be embroidered – and with several thicknesses of tissue laid into the skirt of the garment. If possible, the robe should be stored without any folding, but, if folds have to be made, they

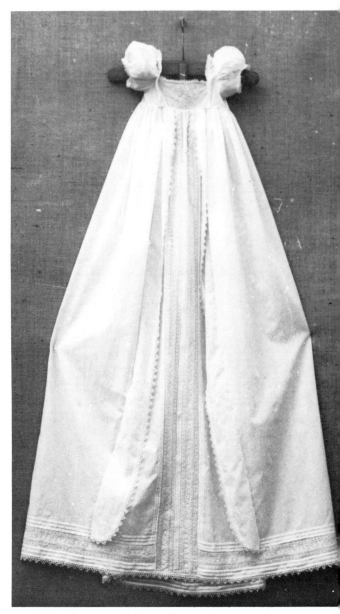

63 *Christening robe relaxing on hanger after storage and before re-use.*

should be loose ones over rolls of tissue.

When the christening robe is again required for use, it may emerge from storage without needing anything more than an hour or so hanging from a padded hanger to allow any slight creases to fall out but, if the fabric seems limp, then its appearance will be improved by starching. Use only rice starch (ordinary old-fashioned Robin starch, for example, is suitable) but never use any spray-on or plastic starch or stiffener on an old fabric. A very thin solution of starch should be sufficient. Ironing, if needed, should be done with a lightweight iron at the lowest heat setting which will achieve a smooth crisp effect (generally about 100°C, 212°F).

After the christening the robe should be washed again with the greatest care, to remove the starch and any trace of soiling, and the garment returned to storage.

Wedding veils

A wedding veil, like a christening robe, may be a family heirloom which is required for occasional wearing. If the veil has been stored, clean and in good order, either loosely folded over rolls of tissue paper or rolled around a cylinder with plenty of acid-free tissue paper, it should emerge, when required, needing nothing more than shaking out so that it is ready to be worn again.But if it is in need of washing and some repairing, its size makes it rather a problem. The problem, however, is not in the washing but in the space needed for drying. What is needed is a clear space, with a piece of polythene stretched and pinned in place on it, both slightly larger than the veil when it is stretched out to its full size. If those two requirements can be met, the next step is to spread the veil out and examine it carefully for any weak or damaged areas. Extensive repair of a valuable veil should be the work of an expert, but minor tidying up is not too difficult and the veil can usually be arranged, when it is worn, so that small defects or repairs are hidden in folds. Fine net can be used to patch or strengthen weak areas, using a small embroidery frame as described in Chapter 8 on conservation. Be sure that any patching or tiny darns are made with stitching at exactly the right tension so that there is no pull or drag on surrounding areas. Pay particular attention to the condition of the edges of the veil; if they are fragile or seem likely to tear or break, repair them, either with an edging of fine net or oversewing.

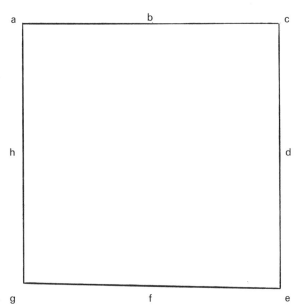

64 *Diagram of folding sequence for use when preparing wedding veil for washing.*

Having made the piece as whole as possible, it will be necessary to reduce it to a manageable size for washing. Spread the veil out again, smooth, flat and in its proper shape, and fold it up for washing. Consulting the accompanying diagram, bring one side edge to the centre (AG to BF), and then the other side edge to the centre to meet the first (CE to BF). Next, bring the bottom edge up to the centre (GE to HD) and then the top edge to the centre (AC to HD) and continue in this fashion until the folded parcel is small enough to fit comfortably into the available washing vessel. When the right size is achieved, tack the square all round using fine mercerised sewing cotton or silk sewing thread and large loose stitches. Now wash the piece, supported on a piece of monofilament screening, using the washing method we have given. Have sufficient distilled or de-ionised water to be able to retain a small quantity even after the thorough final rinsing. Lift the parcel, still on its screening, from the washing vessel, pat with a towel to remove a little of the water, and carry it to the prepared drying area, the clear space covered with the large piece of polythene. Put

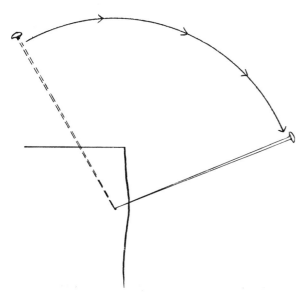

65 *Method of pinning to achieve slight tension in drying wedding veil.*

the wet parcel of veil in the centre of the drying area with its folds facing upwards and cut the threads holding the parcel together. The purpose of the careful folding is now revealed as it is unfolded. It helps to have two people to unfold the veil, one taking each side. Open out each fold and, with care, the veil will come out to its full size without difficulty and without having to be pulled out to shape. Once the veil is opened out completely, wet the veil all over again using the distilled or de-ionised water which you have kept back for the purpose by sprinkling it all over until it almost floats on the polythene. It will now be possible to pull it gently and safely into its proper shape. Continue until all is straight and true, paying attention to the borders, especially if these have a pattern of curves or scallops. Pin the veil into position all round the edge, using brass lace pins. Put each in firmly, with the head slanting towards the centre of the veil, and then lever it so that it slants away from the veil and produces just a little tension which, if it is the same all over, will ensure that the veil dries in its correct shape and pattern. The veil will dry overnight; make sure

that it does so undisturbed. This same method can be used in the washing of lace tablecloths and bedspreads.

Ironing

After washing, most pieces, if straightened when wet and allowed to dry in the correct way, should not require ironing. If, however, some ironing is deemed necessary, the temperature of a lightweight iron should not be allowed to rise above 100°C (212°F) – that is the *cool* or lowest setting on most irons. The application of heat to fibres, particularly in pressing material into sharp folds, is potentially very damaging. If folds are essential to the structure of a textile object – say in the form of pleats – it is better to press these gently into position with the fingers while the fabric is damp and to hold them in place on the melinex-covered softboard with upright brass lace pins, so that the fibres can dry in the required way. Fabrics pleated or folded when first made seem to retain the memory of this and, with a little encouragement, will fall naturally into the desired position.

Stains

Any stains or spots which remain on old textiles after washing are best left alone, even though there are various commercial preparations available for removing them. This is because the chemicals which these removing agents contain will almost certainly weaken old and fragile fibres, and it is far better to have a spot than a weakened area, or even a hole needing repairs which would easily prove more obtrusive than the original mark.

Many bleaching methods are hazardous for old textiles and the result may not be worth the risk involved. The old *natural* method of bleaching by drying in sunlight is also potentially damaging to old fabrics. White lace, in particular, may have acquired a yellow tinge by the time it is old but, providing it is clean, the mellowed effect of age is surely preferable to having lace which has been bleached white but weakened.

To summarise, washing is not only an irreversible process, it is also a potentially destructive one, and the washing of an old textile should be undertaken only after tests, and then using great care. There are many things that can go wrong. Success will be the result of anticipating dangers and taking steps to avoid them, and doing everything carefully and with forethought. Experience will bring confidence, but also the realisation that one can never afford to be careless or casual.

66 *Washing a modern sisal hanging. (This hanging, 'The Eagle', is by Tadek Beutlich). A smaller bath has been created on the tiled floor of the large tapestry washing room by building an area covered with polythene sheeting. The darker piece of the wall on the right leads to the drain and can be easily moved. Soft water and all facilities are to hand.*

OPPOSITE ABOVE
67 *The hanging is drying. Damp air is being drawn into one of the hoses of the de-humidifier and discharged outside through an open window, while dry air is blown onto the hanging from the other hose; no heat is used during the drying process. The hanging is being supported by a row of metal trestles and across a piece of monofilament screening so that it is raised from the floor.*

OPPOSITE
68 *The Eagle is hanging clean and ready to be collected. (It is part of the collection of the Council for National Academic Awards).*

7

Tapestries

The arras, rich with horseman, hawk and hound,
Fluttered in the besieging wind's uproar
And the long carpets rose along the dusty floor.
John Keats, *Eve of St Agnes*

A tapestry is probably the largest and most valuable single textile that anyone can own, and tapestries are the most numerous of all the really old textiles in this country. Tapestries are very much a part of British history, although the number of tapestries actually woven here has been relatively small. Most of the tapestries to be seen now are those covering the walls of castles, country houses and other large buildings, or hanging in museums and art galleries, although there are some still in private ownership. Tapestries are often in series or groups with a common theme, for it was quite customary to buy sets of tapestries with which to line the walls of specific rooms, and generally the subjects they depict are of a heroic nature and scope in keeping with their great size. Favourite subjects were scenes of battle or hunting, illustrations of religious, mythological or allegorical stories, and later ones showing classical or pastoral scenes, often of an idyllic nature, with flower-strewn leafy glades and distant vistas of hilltop castles or idealised scenes of country life.

The quality of tapestries varies enormously both in technique of weaving and design. While the weaving of some may be rather loose and coarse, those which were made by later weavers in some of the very famous European workshops are of very fine, close work. Many mediaeval tapestries which have survived were woven almost entirely of wool, but weavers working later used much more silk, both for highlights in the actual designs and also for quite large areas of sky. Metal threads had been much used in the

textiles of the Middle Ages, and had probably helped to give the name to the famous Field of the Cloth of Gold of Henry VIII's day, who was well known for his love of and ownership of many tapestries. These metal threads continued to be used in some of the more opulent tapestries.

Most tapestries were woven on warps of wool, although linen warps were used in some small tapestries. The weaving technique employed is one in which the weft threads are pushed or beaten closely together during weaving so that they cover the warp threads completely, producing a firm fabric. But, by examining a hanging tapestry a little more closely, it can be seen that the warp threads – the strongest and most durable threads in the tapestry which go right through the weaving without a break – are going across the tapestry horizontally, which does not seem right if the tapestry is to be hung for its greatest safety. In fact, the tapestry was woven sideways-on to the design, a difficult technique even for those incredible craftsmen, the master weavers. Of course there was a reason. The width of any piece of weaving is governed by the width of the loom. Warp threads can be of any length but their number is restricted by just how many can be accommodated side by side in the loom. Anyone who buys material by the yard or metre realises this because cloth is sold in different specified widths, depending on the size of the loom on which it was woven, but one can buy almost any length required. One of the original purposes of

69 *Professional tapestry conservation in progress. Bare warps, some of them broken, can be seen in an area where the silk weft has been damaged and has fallen out. At the far right, by the darkheaded pin, a badly stitched up slit will need restitching. Above and to the left of the scissors, the couching method of conservation, which preserves any remaining silk weft, has been completed.*

tapestries was to line the walls of draughty stone castles and palaces, and sets of tapestries which were always very prized were carried around by royalty and noblemen as they moved from one residence to another. As the width of the loom, which carries the warp threads, dictated one dimension of a tapestry, length was the only measurement that could be varied and, since a design in weaving is achieved by changing the colours of the weft threads, the design was woven sideways to the required length. This technique has persisted, and has resulted in

problems which those caring for tapestries have to solve. The history of tapestries makes fascinating reading and we have included one of the best small books on the subject in the reading list at the end of this book.

Assessing the condition

A hanging tapestry which does not show any obvious sign of deterioration will hold together, almost from force of habit, for a very long time, providing it is not disturbed. As it is a textile it is prone to the usual forms of deterioration we have detailed, but, unless it is decided to go ahead with proper conservation in the form of professional cleaning and any other treatment which may be proved necessary, our advice would be that it is far better to leave the tapestry alone and not risk damage by disturbing it, until such time as it can be properly conserved, although an advisory visit from a trained tapestry conservator would obviously be a safeguard. Obvious effects of deterioration will occur when any of the fibres become so weak that they finally break and part. This will cause the tapestry to sag in that area, putting strain on other parts which, if they are also weak, will break; from this point on damage will continue at an accelerating rate. The silk threads in a tapestry are likely to deteriorate and become brittle before the woollen ones, except in the case of dark wools that have been weakened by dyeing as in the aforementioned example of the dark outlines in Gothic tapestries.

There are certain first aid measures which can be carefully undertaken by the non-professional on the spot, provided that the deterioration is noticed at an early stage. Some of this work can be done while the tapestry is still hanging. The weakest parts in the actual weave of a tapestry are the slits which occur where two colours in the design meet. During the weaving, changing from one colour to another was sometimes achieved by twisting the weft threads of the two colours round each other; this makes the strongest join. Otherwise, one coloured weft thread was taken up to and round a warp thread and then back again, while the other, adjoining, colour was taken up to and round the next warp and back again. This method of changing from one colour to another in the weft makes a slit. When the tapestry weaving was finished, these slits were sewn up, generally with silk. When the silk perishes and the stitching breaks away, the weight of the tapestry causes the slits to gape open which puts a lot of strain on the rest of the piece. It is possible to sew up gaping slits while the tapestry is still hanging, provided the surrounding areas are in a good condition.

Use a fine, curved needle and linen thread in an appropriate, unobtrusive colour. It is usual to make the stitches so that they are straight across on the right side and slanting on the wrong side, as we have illustrated. Be very careful not to stitch through a warp thread as this will cause pull and strain. Do not let the stitches catch into the lining. A small pair of pliers is a help in getting the needle through the work. First aid of

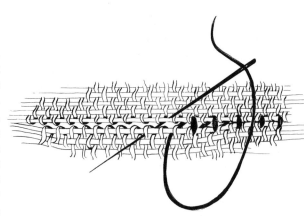

70 *Sewing up a slit, being careful not to stitch through a warp thread and to keep the straight stitches on the right side of the tapestry. If the tapestry is in a frame, the stitching would be done upwards and away from the conservator.*

this kind, done as preventive conservation as soon as the damage is noticed, will save the tapestry from possible further strain and distortion, but no attempt should ever be made to sew up any broken areas in the actual weaving. The only acceptable first aid sewing is to replace broken threads which join slits. If any doubt exists, do nothing until professional advice has been given.

The sky area at the top of a tapestry, especially of tapestries of the seventeenth century and after, was often woven almost entirely with a silk weft. As silk is liable to earlier deterioration than wool and is always less strong, this meant that the weakest area was called upon to take the greatest weight, and the condition of that part of the tapestry should always be watched for signs of deterioration. This is not always easy or obvious as the area in question is generally well above eye level. Responsible care of tapestries should, therefore, allow for periodic inspection at close quarters but no attempt should be made to do any remedial work in the silk areas of a hanging tapestry.

Washing and conservation work on tapestries should always be entrusted to a trained and qualified tapestry conservator. Tapestry conservation is a very time-consuming process and the more extensive the work required, the greater the cost. Therefore, the earlier the trouble is detected, the less damage will have been caused, and the less time – and therefore money – will have to be spent on treatment. If the expert's assessment is that the tapestry is safe to hang for some time, possibly suggesting that the slits are sewn up and vacuum cleaning through screening is done, then that advice is reasonably easy to follow, but if it is necessary to take the tapestry down, then it will have to be decided how and by whom the tapestry is to be removed from the wall.

If you want to keep a deteriorating tapestry on show while you are waiting for professional help, then the tapestry can be taken down and first aid support given to the weak areas by using the lining as a support, stitching the tapestry to the lining in the weak areas. Use linen thread in an unobtrusive colour and take long stitches, being careful not to stitch through a warp thread. The tension of the stitches is important because if they are too loose they serve no purpose, and if they are too tight they will pull and distort the tapestry. This is strictly a short-term first aid measure and should be supervised by a trained and qualified conservator. Full professional conservation treatment should be given to the tapestry as soon as possible.

Taking a tapestry down from a wall

Several people will be required to move a tapestry safely from a wall. Even a small one can be surprisingly heavy and no part should be allowed to be without continual support throughout the entire moving operation. Remember, too, that the tapestry will almost certainly be dusty and dirty and could be brittle.

We would never recommend rolling a brittle tapestry sideways off the wall, even if special equipment and manpower were available for this method, because in rolling sideways the top edge, with its fastenings, becomes increasingly bulky and this, combined with the heavy weight of the tapestry, will inevitably cause sagging which, in turn, will damage brittle silk.

A safer way to take a tapestry down is to roll it upwards from the bottom, on to either a wooden

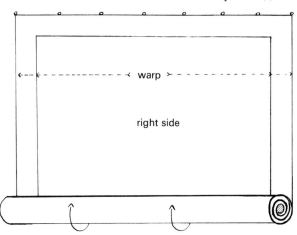

71 *Rolling up a tapestry to remove it from the wall.*

pole, a cylinder of cardboard or a piece of plastic drainpipe. Whatever is used should be strong enough not to bend or break with the weight of the tapestry, and smooth enough not to damage it. It will be necessary to have at least one person at each side of the tapestry to do the rolling up on to the cylinder, with step ladders to reach the top and, if the tapestry is large and heavy, more people in between to help take the weight. Starting at the bottom, roll the tapestry carefully up on to the roller until it almost reaches the top where the piece is fixed to the wall. Release whatever is fastening it to the wall and bring the rolled and supported tapestry carefully to the ground. If the tapestry has been attached to the wall by the use of touch-and-close fastener, releasing it will be very easy; otherwise there may be rings to lift from hooks, poppers to undo or (though one would deplore this) nails to take out. If the tapestry is hanging on a hoist, letting it down and rolling it on to a cylinder as it reaches the ground will be the easiest way of all. The hoist and touch-and-close fastener methods of hanging are described later in this chapter as part of the re-hanging process after lining a tapestry.

When the rolled tapestry is down, unroll it very carefully on to the floor so that the back of the tapestry is uppermost. If the tapestry is going for immediate further cleaning or conser-

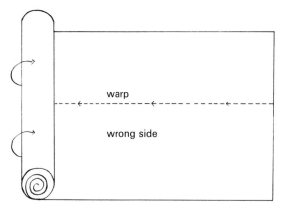

72 *Re-rolling a tapestry for storage or transportation.*

vation treatment, no cleaning need be done at this stage but, if it is to be stored for any length of time, it is a good idea to clean the back of the tapestry by careful use of a vacuum cleaner through monofilament screening. The next operation is to re-roll the tapestry on to the roller covered with acid-free tissue paper (if it is made of cardboard), but this time it should be rolled so that the stronger warp threads go round the roller, in contrast to the way it was rolled when it was taken down. If re-rolling is not done the weft threads are left stretched, and damage occurs because old fibres are seldom elastic enough to resume their original length after stretching. To roll the tapestry with the warps round the roller means taking the roller round to the side of the design as in the drawing. In this second rolling, the right side of the tapestry should again be on the outside. If the tapestry is to be stored for any length of time, vacuum the right side as the tapestry is being rolled, again through screening. Once rolled, the tapestry can be covered with a dust sheet and stored lying horizontally on its roller, in a cool, dry, dark place, until it is required for re-hanging or conservation. A stored and rolled tapestry should always be kept lying down lengthwise so that it is safely supported, and the roll should never be allowed to stand upright on one end.

Lining

Tapestries should always be lined, because a well-fitted lining provides support and also prevents dust and dirt collecting on the back of the tapestry. Anyone who examines the reverse side of an unlined tapestry will see that there appear to be hundreds of strands of wool and silk hanging there that have gathered dust. If one knows nothing of tapestry weaving these ends look rather unnecessary and untidy. They are, however, the ends of the weft threads left by the weavers as part of the weaving process which involved a number of changes of colour and pattern in the design. These weft ends should never be cut off; even their length is critical and they should be left strictly alone. If any of them are short-ended or broken off, then the short end may work its way through to the right side of the tapestry and the weaving will gradually come undone.

An examination of the reverse side of a tapestry will also reveal how much the colours on the right side have faded through exposure to light. There was once a quite serious restoration attempt to recapture the original appearance of a faded tapestry by turning it back to front and taking all the loose ends back through the tapestry to the other side but, apart from the considerable difficulties encountered in that process and the peculiar effect made by all the figures on the tapestry appearing left-handed, it was then realised that the colours would inevitably fade again, and the attempt was not repeated.

Lining a tapestry, while quite an undertaking because of its size, could be done by competent needleworkers, particularly those with experience in the lining of curtains. This work might be a project for a group working in a stately home or in a similar situation. No attempt should be made to line or re-line a tapestry unless it is clean and in good condition.

First, decide how much lining is required. Tapestries are best lined with linen or brown

73 *Old man's head in tapestry – reverse side showing weft ends.*

74 *Old man's head in tapestry – right side.*

holland and this should be shrunk before use (see drawing), so calculations of the amount required must take into account the loss through shrinking. Supposing the tapestry measures 12 × 10 ft (360 × 300 cm); the lining, after shrinking, would need to measure at least 13 × 11 ft (390 × 330 cm). If the lining has not been allowed to shrink before it is applied, it could do so afterwards, even by exposure to a damp atmosphere, and this would cause pull and strain on the tapestry. A larger lining is needed if the tapestry is of a coarse or loose weave because the lining will have to be more loosely applied to make sure that it cannot pull or distort the tapestry.

Work out the amount of lining required, add a generous amount in both length and width for shrinking and buy the linen. Linen sold by the yard/metre is not very wide as a rule, so several widths will have to be joined to make the lining of a large tapestry. These joins should run vertically on the lining.

Shrinking

We find that the easiest way to shrink the linen is to do so while it is still in its uncut length as bought from the shop. Prepare a bath of warm water and lower the length of linen into it in concertina-like folds so that there is, eventually, a folded square of linen lying at the bottom of the bath. Allow this to soak for some hours. The water, which will have probably become quite brown, should be drained away and the linen covered again, this time with hot water. Drain and replenish the water several times more, allowing the linen to soak undisturbed in each lot of water. When the water remains clear, the soaking can stop. Drain the water away and lift the linen on to a pole or board across the bath and let it drip for a while. Then lift it out and undo it on a flat surface, for example a lawn which has been covered with some protective material, smoothing it out as flat as possible. When it is almost dry, fold it carefully and put it in a press under a board on which there are as

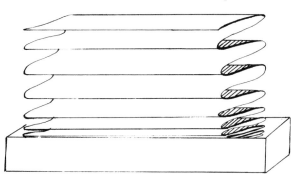

75 *Lowering linen into bath to allow shrinking.*

many evenly distributed weights as possible and leave until the linen is quite dry. If the material has been kept smooth throughout the whole operation, no ironing will be needed. Once it is dry, although it will have shrunk, it will be just like material straight from the shop. Ironing is to be avoided because it is almost impossible to iron material without stretching and distorting it to some extent.

Next cut the linen into the lengths required for the lining and join these together at the selvedges with machine or hand stitching.

76 *Method of joining selvedges of lining to make required width.*

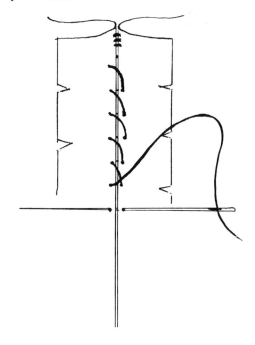

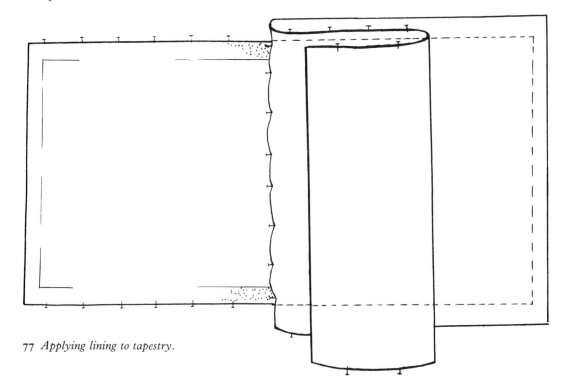

77 *Applying lining to tapestry.*

When each seam is finished, snip the selvedges every 6 in (15 cm) or so and check carefully that there is no puckering along the seams. The seams can be pressed open with the fingers. The lining is now ready to be attached to the tapestry and the method used is very similar to that for curtain lining, except that there are more lines of stitching made in attaching tapestry linings in order to provide more support.

Attaching the lining

Supposing we are still dealing with a tapestry of about 12 × 10 ft (360 × 300 cm), the clean tapestry should be placed on a flat surface, wrong side uppermost and as straight and smooth as possible. Ideally, the flat surface should be a table, or tables of the same height put together to make the right size. When dealing with a large tapestry this may not be possible, and a clean floor may well provide the only space large enough. For most people, working on the floor is extremely tiring and it is wise to take this into consideration in order not to work under these conditions for too long at any one time, as this

can result in mistakes due to strain. The corners of handwoven textiles such as tapestries are very seldom at exactly 90° and, once the piece is laid flat, it may be obvious that the piece is not a true rectangle or even that the edges are not really quite straight. Put a straight row of pins horizontally across the top edge of the tapestry, just below the edge of the weaving. You can get a straight line the way gardeners do by stretching a cord between two points. Find the exact centre of this line of pins and then make another row of pins at an exact right angle to the top row, going down the centre of the tapestry from the top to the bottom edge. This vertical line of pins may, or may not, be exactly parallel to the edges of the tapestry but should be quite straight. Now place the prepared lining on top of the tapestry, right side uppermost, putting the centre top of the lining to the centre top of the tapestry and the centre bottom of the lining to the last pin in the vertical row down the tapestry. Smooth the lining out to make sure that it overlaps the tapestry on each side.

See that there are about 2 in (5 cm) of lining

78 *Locking stitch for attaching the lining vertically.*

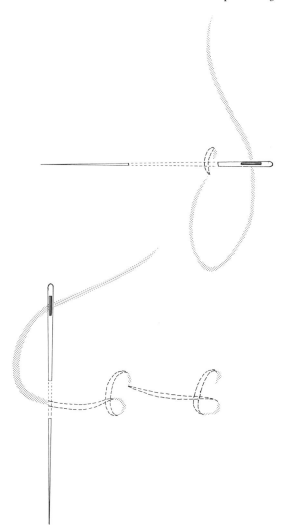

79 *Horizontal locking stitches for attaching the lining.*

above the top of the tapestry and that the lining covers the tapestry completely. Turn the lining back on itself along the central vertical row of pins in a straight line and pin the fold of the lining to the tapestry down the centre line of pins, starting at the top and easing the lining between each pin by pushing it a little towards the top before putting in the next pin, so that, although the tapestry still lies quite flat, the lining is very slightly eased as the pins are inserted. A very finely woven tapestry can take a lining that is quite closely fitted, but a loosely woven tapestry must have a loosely fitted lining.

Once this row of pins is in place, the lining can be stitched to the tapestry, using linen thread and a locking stitch, which is a loose buttonhole stitch. Each stitch takes up only one warp thread of the tapestry so that it will be covered by the weft. The stitches should be about 1½ in (4 cm) apart and should finish about 4 in (10 cm) from the bottom of the tapestry. Turn the lining back again so that it completely covers the tapestry and again fold it back on itself about 13 in (32.5 cm) from the first fold on the left-hand

side of the centre fold. On the tapestry, measure 12 in (30 cm) from the centre and pin the lining by its fold down a line at this point parallel to the centre, again easing the lining between the pins. The extra 1 in (2.5 cm) of width between the two lines of stitching will also ensure that the lining will not drag or pull the tapestry.

Repeat this operation on the left-hand side three times more (five lines of stitching) and then make five similar lines on the right-hand side of the centre line, remembering to remove

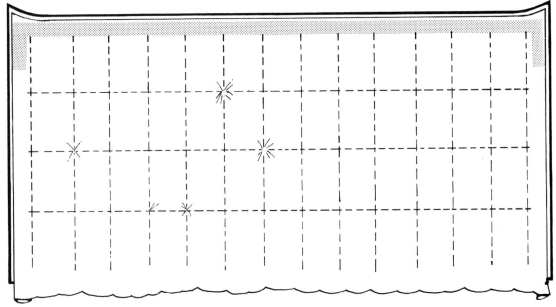

80 *Back of lined tapestry showing pattern of locking stitches.*

all marking pins, especially those marking the original centre line, before locking on the lining. When the vertical lines of stitching are complete, make horizontal lines, about 12 in (30 cm) apart, across the lining. These lines are made with stitches catching the lining and a warp thread of the tapestry and then running the needle between the lining and the tapestry for about 1½ in (4 cm) before coming to the surface of the lining to make another stitch, through the lining and round a warp thread of the tapestry.

These vertical and horizontal lines of stitching will give the effect of squares when you look at the lined side of the textile. The sides and top of the lining should be turned under and caught to the edges of the tapestry with slip stitches. Do not, however, sew up the bottom hem of the lining until the lined tapestry has been allowed to hang for a day or two, so that it can be seen if there is any drag or pull between lining and tapestry which will have to be relieved, and also to let the piece settle and drop if it wishes. After a few days make any necessary adjustments, turn up the hem of the lining and slip-stitch into place. This method is used for the lining of any

hanging textile although, of course, measurements will differ and it may not always be necessary to have so many lines of vertical locking stitches or any horizontal lines at all.

Hanging a tapestry

The best and safest way to hang a textile is by the use of Velcro, the contact fastener. The width of the Velcro chosen should be dictated by the size of the hanging, a strip 2 in (5 cm) wide being sufficiently strong even for a heavy tapestry. A revised method of attaching Velcro is proving better than the former one in which the Velcro was sewn straight onto the lined tapestry.

Measure the top edge of the lined tapestry and cut a strip of Velcro to that length. Next cut two pieces of 1 in (2.5 cm) wide cotton twill tape but make these the length of the Velcro *plus* ½ in (13 mm) to allow a turning of ¼ in (6 mm) at each end.

Stretch one piece of the tape out straight along a table or other flat surface and then place the second piece of tape exactly below it, leaving a small gap between the two tapes. Separate the two component pieces of the Velcro by pulling them apart and taking the strip with the soft fluffy surface, place it, fluffy side uppermost, on

81 *Illustration to show method of attaching Velcro
(touch-and-close fastener) to lining of tapestry.
Velcro in position on top of two lengths of tape,
machine stitched along top and bottom edges of
Velcro and again about $\frac{1}{2}$ in (13 mm) away from the
edges. The top surface in the illustration would be
attached to a wooden batten where the piece is to
hang.*

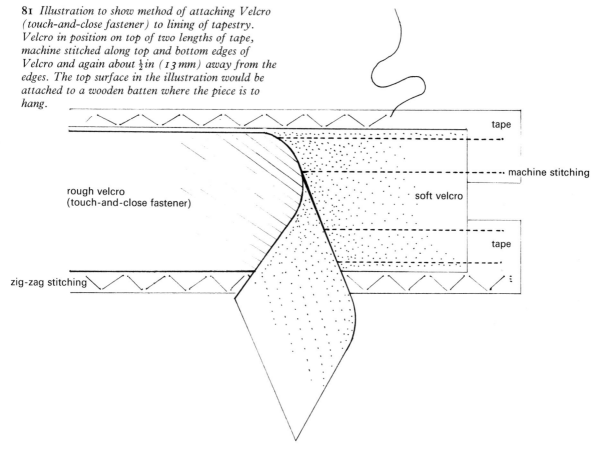

tape

machine stitching

rough velcro
(touch-and-close fastener)

soft velcro

tape

zig-zag stitching

82 *Reverse side of demonstration piece shown in figure 83 showing position of tapes and Velcro before stitching.*

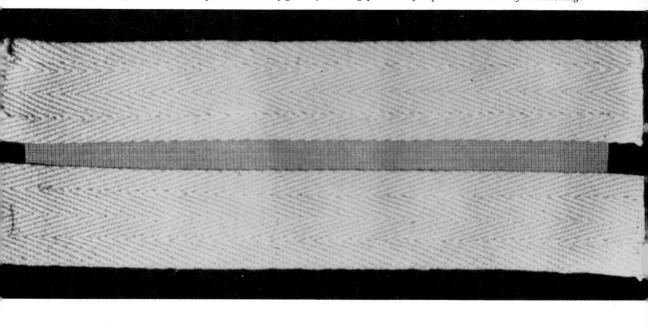

83 *Velcro (and tapes) attached on top of lined tapestry by zig-zag stitches going through tape, lining and tapestry. (Demonstration piece).*

top of the two pieces of tape. Position it so that all three pieces are straight and parallel, with $\frac{1}{4}$ in (6 mm) of the top tape appearing above the strip of Velcro, $\frac{1}{4}$ in (6 mm) of the lower tape appearing below the Velcro and the extra $\frac{1}{4}$ in (6 mm) length of each tape protruding beyond each end of the Velcro. Pin or tack into position and machine-stitch to secure, making four lines of stitching in all. The top and bottom lines of stitching should be made into the Velcro's narrow lengthwise edgings and the top and bottom $\frac{1}{4}$ in (6 mm) of tape with the other two lines of stitching about $\frac{1}{2}$ in (13 mm) below that,

above the bottom and below the top lines respectively. Finally, turn under the $\frac{1}{4}$ in (6 mm) cut edges of the tape ends and machine across the tapes and Velcro.

Pin or tack the prepared Velcro/tapes (fluffy side of Velcro outwards) along the top edge of the lined tapestry and then secure, using a cotton or linen thread and a strong needle. Make stitches through tape, lining and tapestry along the top piece of tape. The stitches used should produce a zig-zag pattern on the Velcro side and small, vertical, unobtrusive stitches each going over one warp thread on the front of the tapestry. Repeat this line of stitching along the bottom piece of tape, again going through tape, lining and tapestry.

Fix the corresponding strip of Velcro, which

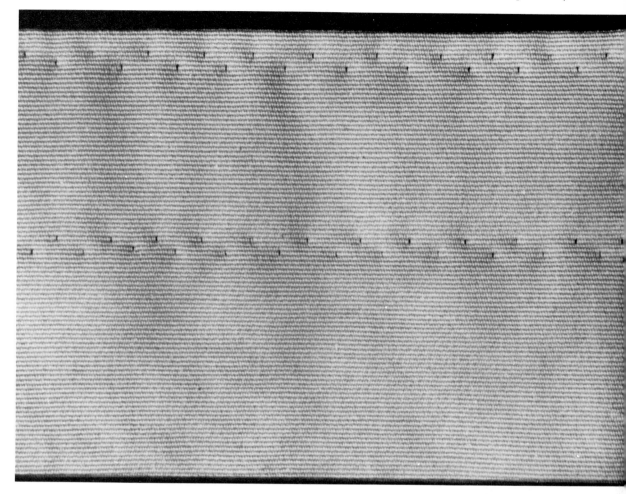

84 *Vertical stitches, each going over one warp thread on right side of tapestry of demonstration piece.*

has a rather rough, hard surface, to a wooden batten, using one row of tin tacks along the top edge of the Velcro and one row along the middle, leaving the bottom edge of the Velcro strip free. Now fix the batten to the wall where the textile will hang, remembering to choose a position away from direct light and any source of heat, such as a radiator.

By pressing the two strips of Velcro together, the textile will hang evenly supported along its whole width. It can easily be adjusted to hang to the best possible advantage. As already mentioned, the corners of handwoven pieces are

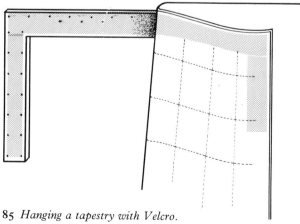

85 *Hanging a tapestry with Velcro.*

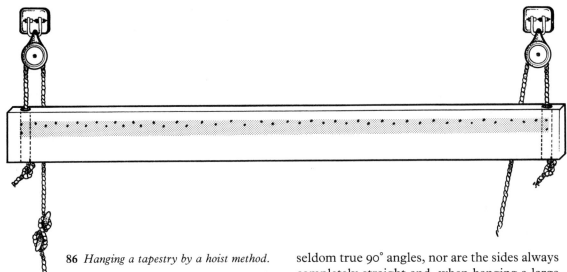

86 *Hanging a tapestry by a hoist method.*

87 *Fragment of tapestry, possibly woven at Tourney in about 1500. 'Jacob's Dream' – before conservation.*

seldom true 90° angles, nor are the sides always completely straight and, when hanging a large handwoven textile in other ways, such as with rings along the top or by using a sleeve and a rod, it is often quite difficult to get the piece to hang straight enough to be visually acceptable; the Velcro method makes adjustment easy. A small, but important point, too, is that the hanging can easily be removed for cleaning or in an emer-

88 *'Jacob's Dream' – after conservation.*

89 *Detail of the 'Jacob's Dream' tapestry after conservation.*

gency such as a fire. If the hanging is really very large and heavy it may be advisable to put additional strips of Velcro, and corresponding battens, at right angles down each of the sides for about 2 ft (60 cm) from the top for greater support, attached in the same way as described above.

If it is known that the help available to hang or take down a tapestry will always be limited, or if it is anticipated that the tapestries on display may often be changed around, it would be worthwhile to install a hoist system. This would mean that, instead of nailing the Velcro to a batten fixed on the wall, it would be put on to a length of wood which could be raised and lowered by a simple system of pulleys. Thus the tapestry could be attached or detached while the cylinder on which it is rolled is still on the ground, and raised or lowered safely and easily.

Vacuum cleaning

It is possible to clean the surface of a hanging tapestry, which is in good condition, by a method mentioned already, using a vacuum cleaner and monofilament screening. The screening can be used in lengths, held either vertically or horizontally and moved along as each area of the hanging is cleaned, passing the nozzle of the vacuum cleaner over it. If a number of tapestries are to be cleaned in this way, it would be worthwhile attaching the screening to smooth wooden battens to give rigidity so that it could be more easily moved along. Several people may be needed – to hold the screening in position, to hold the cleaner, to direct the nozzle (which should be fitted to the longest reaching attachment of the cleaner) and, in the case of a really large tapestry, step ladders would have to be used to reach the top of the hanging. Care is needed at all stages, but this cleaning need not be done too frequently and then should only be attempted on tapestries in good condition which the removal of surface dust and dirt would help to maintain.

Carpets and rugs

Some carpets and rugs with a flat surface may have been woven in almost exactly the same way as a tapestry. First aid in sewing up slits in the weaving would, therefore, be applicable and the method is the same as that used on tapestries. Worn or fragile areas should be strengthened by applying patches of linen to the wrong side of the carpet or rug with careful stitching, using linen thread in an unobtrusive colour and taking care always to stitch between, and not through, warp threads.

The edges of carpets are frequently the first parts to show signs of wear, and these can be strengthened by oversewing. Study the way the edges have been finished originally and try to copy this, being careful not to stitch too closely or too tightly because this will only cause strain and damage. Fringes on carpets or rugs are usually the ends of warp threads, possibly knotted or woven with a special finishing border. The fringes become worn, and if this deterioration is allowed to continue it will eventually result in the unravelling of the weaving. If tape or webbing is stitched along the edge on the wrong side this will give support, and the piece will stay safe for a longer period. The edges of pile carpets and rugs can also benefit from similar attention. Never use any adhesive tape or binding on valuable floor coverings.

8

Conservation and restoration

But what is past my help, is past my care.
Beaumont and Fletcher, *The Double Marriage*

As every textile presents its own conservation problems, rules for treatment are almost impossible to formulate beyond agreeing that most old textiles will need cleaning in some form, not necessarily washing; after that, many will also need some support and, if they are to be displayed, will need to be made as attractive as possible.

We have tried to show in Chapter 6 that cleaning old textiles requires a different approach from that normally used for domestic fabrics. Similarly, the techniques used in the conservation and restoration of old textiles are different from those used in mending everyday materials and making-up or embroidering new fabrics. The expert needleworker may find that

90 *This child's tunic from a Coptic burial ground is more than 1,000 years old. Seen here before conservation.*

he or she has to learn to resist the temptation to do too much sewing when trying to save an old textile and would, in fact, be well advised to regard textile conservation as a skill requiring the adoption of a completely new technique and outlook. Successful treatment is achieved by doing just enough to make an object safe for display, storage or re-use and to make it appear whole and looking right. Although, as with washing and cleaning, it is wise to send any textile which has artistic or historic importance to a professional for treatment, the appearance and safety of many other treasured textiles can, with care, be improved.

Conservation requires that everything that is original on an object be retained, and nothing added. Restoration, on the other hand, implies a degree of repair so that the piece not only looks as nearly as it did originally, but it may even be made strong enough for further use. One would conserve a piece for display as part of a collection, as was the case with the piece of Coptic weaving illustrated earlier, but one would restore the old canvas-work or tapestry cover of a chair which is intended to be used again.

Attaching the textile to a support

The most effective support one can give an old and fragile textile is to back it with a suitable material, and choosing the type of backing is of great importance. It should be compatible with the textile it will support and suitable in weight, weave, colour and type of fibre. Again, there are no rules to govern the choice of supporting materials except to acknowledge that natural materials have an affinity for each other, as have man-made fibres.

OPPOSITE ABOVE
92 *Same area after conservation when the garment was given support by applying it to a suitable material.*

OPPOSITE
93 *Hood before conservation. Note decorative motifs incorporated in the weaving.*

91 *Detail in neck area after washing.*

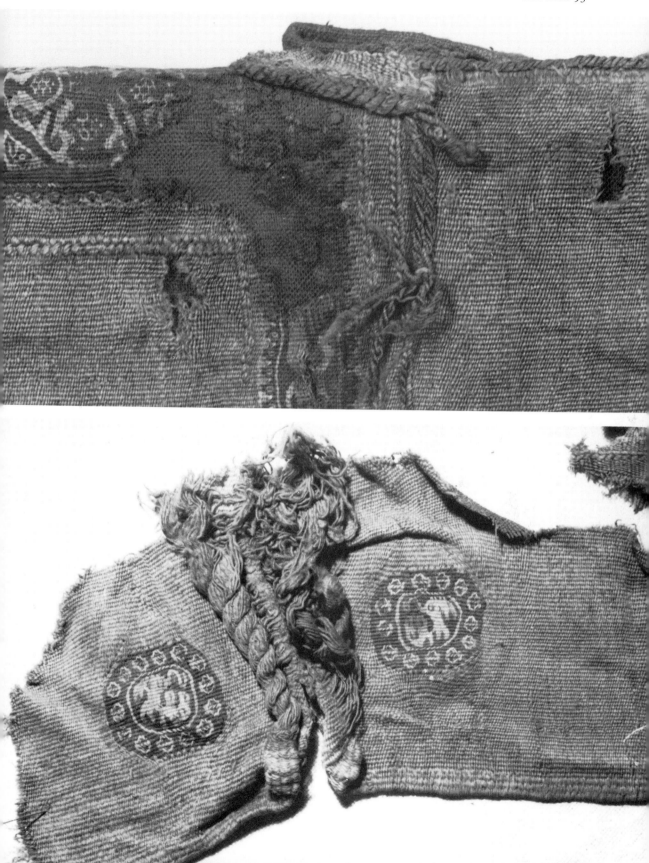

94 *The hood folded back, after conservation. Its shape was made up by the supporting fabric, which also supplied the original shape of the missing area on the right, and backs small holes on the left-hand side of the picture.*

The way to apply an old textile to its support is by first mounting the supporting material in an embroidery frame. In fact the use of an embroidery frame is almost essential in textile conservation because the tension can be kept constant, handling reduced to a minimum and the work left safely covered up between sessions of work. The latter is important since textile conservation is something which cannot be hurried; some jobs can take a very long time to complete and this must be accepted.

The type of embroidery frame which is the most useful to have is that which is known in Britain as a tapestry frame.

These can be bought in different sizes measured by the length of the tapes or webbing on the rollers to which the material is stitched. A small frame with webbing of 18 in (45 cm) in length will take material up to 16 in (40 cm) wide, but a really large one such as is used in the conservation of tapestries can be over 20 ft (6 m) wide. Ideally, one would choose a frame of the right size for each job from a large stock, but they are expensive to buy and if only one is to be acquired then it is always better to have the largest that one can afford or has room to use; although it is possible to use a large frame for a narrow piece of material, the reverse will never be the case. A frame with a tape size of 40 in (100 cm) will be large enough to take the supporting material for, say, a canvas-work or tapestry sofa back. It will be found useful to have at least one small frame permanently fitted with a piece of linen with the centre missing, as

95 *Front view of the conserved tunic.*

96 *Back view of the conserved tunic.*

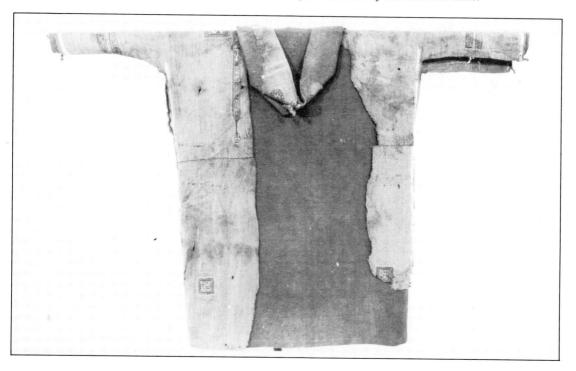

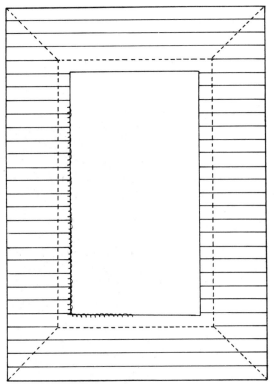

97 *Line drawing of a small frame made from old picture frame, covered with strong linen, with a rectangle cut out and hemmed around in its centre. Small repairs can be done to special areas by pinning the part to be treated across the frame so that the damaged area is held in position for easy stitching.*

in the illustration. This can be an old picture frame or stretcher with the linen attached; its purpose is to provide a frame for small repairs. It can be put under the area to be treated, the textile pinned or sewn to the linen surround and the frame then raised from the table by blocks, or put across a gap of some other kind, so that the necessary stitching can be done through the open centre of the linen. This kind of frame can easily be moved around to treat small areas which do not require the backing of a supporting fabric.

To frame up a supporting material in a larger frame, first see that the centre of each of the strips of webbing or tape on the rollers of the frame is marked. These central marks should be accurate and permanent. Turn the raw edge of the supporting material over about ½ in (13 mm). This fold should be made on the exact straight of the material. Mark the centre of the fold and pin this to the centre of the webbing on the roller. Bring the folded edge of the material to the edge of the webbing and, starting from the centre, oversew them together. When one half is sewn, start at the centre again and oversew the other half. Roll any material surplus to immediate requirement round one roller.

Now attach the other end of the material to the webbing on the other roller in exactly the same way. Put the side pieces into the slots at the ends of each roller and stretch the material out in the frame, inserting the pegs at the sides to keep the material under tension. Make sure that the distance between the top and bottom pegs on each side is exactly the same. The material can be stretched out evenly by putting tapes round the stretchers at the sides and attaching these to the material in the frame. This can be clearly seen in the picture here and, later in this chapter, in that of the frame used in the conservation work on Prince Rupert's coat. These side tapes help to keep the tensions even all over the supporting material in the frame.

The tension of fabrics under treatment is very important in the work of textile conservation and can vary for different needs. For instance, when a small piece of old fabric is being supported, the tension of the old and the supporting material should be the same, neither one pulling the other, and this is comparatively easy to regulate. But when one is dealing with a much larger piece, as would be the case when restoring a piece of upholstery material, there can be difficulties in maintaining the relative tensions; we deal with that problem later.

The correct tension of stitching in conservation is of the greatest importance too. If the stitches are too tight they may cut into the old fabric and cause damage, even more so if they are also too small. If stitches are too loose they will not only be ineffective but will also allow movement between the support and the old textile. Most people tend at first to stitch too tightly, but beware of over-compensating. The

1 *Tapestry woven in Brussels in the seventeenth century. It is one of a series depicting the story of Anthony and Cleopatra. Originally woven with Cleopatra's leg across Anthony's knee, the original weaving of the leg was completely removed in the nineteenth century and the area rewoven as part of Anthony's cloak. Subsequent colour changes in the replacement weaving, however, revealed the outline of Cleopatra's leg.*
(Reproduced by courtesy of The Worshipful Company of Goldsmiths).

2 *Irish tapestry chair back after conservation. From a collection of furniture with Irish tapestry covers which may be seen at Castletown House (near Dublin) which belongs to the Irish Georgian Society.*

3 *The importance of a historic regimental colour made it necessary to replace missing areas with material dyed to recreate the appearance of the original, although as much of the original silk as possible was saved and couched onto a suitable backing fabric. This is a colour of the Royal Sussex Regiment dated prior to 1801.*

4 *The Jeremy Fisher costume from the Royal Ballet's production of 'The Tales of Beatrix Potter', before treatment. The rubber gloves used as hands have also greatly deteriorated.*

5 *After treatment. A new dummy supports the clean costume. Inner gloves protect the perished rubber hands and allow for removable, washable, outer gloves. The costume may be seen at the Sunbury Museum of Childhood, Derbyshire.*

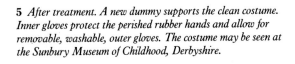

ability to judge correct tension in stitching comes with experience, and most naturally and quickly to those with a feeling for textiles. Having the work in a frame makes it much easier to get the correct tension.

Treatment: examples
What's amiss, I'll strive to mend
And endure what can't be mended.
Isaac Watts, *Good Resolutions*

The actual treatment each object should receive must be decided upon according to its condition and intended future. We have, therefore, chosen to describe the treatment of several different objects or groups of objects, and hope in this way to give as wide a view as possible of what can be done.

Piece of coptic weaving
The conservation of the piece of Coptic weaving illustrated earlier after framing (figure 25) gives our first example. Part of the weaving technique used in making this object is similar to that used when making towelling and, as the piece dried after washing, each loop was carefully pulled out so that all the loops dried straight and separate from each other. When the piece was quite dry, it was applied to a piece of coarse linen which had been stretched in an embroidery frame to an even tension. First, the piece was pinned in place with entomological pins, making sure that the warp and weft threads of both the Coptic weaving and the linen were straight. Entomological pins are long and very fine and are invaluable for holding down fragile pieces and loose threads before stitching, being so thin that they can be inserted between the threads of even delicate materials, leaving no hole at all when they are withdrawn.

Once the Coptic piece was pinned in place, a reel of button thread was chosen in a colour as near that of the supporting material as possible, and a short length cut off for use. This particular make of cable-twisted thread, now, sadly, no longer obtainable, would untwist into three strands, each of which would further untwist into three more strands, making nine in all.

Using a very fine needle and one strand (one ninth of the button thread), the Coptic piece was sewn onto the supporting material all round the edge and round the missing areas. Stitches were also made to fasten down all the loose and damaged threads in the Coptic piece. Once this had been done, the linen supporting the old textile was taken from the embroidery frame, cut into a square and hemmed around. In this way the Coptic piece was given a recognisable shape, missing areas were less obvious and its fragile fibres were supported by the strong linen.

Should a similar undertaking be done today, in the absence of button thread from which to obtain such a fine stitching thread, a fine but strong silk thread would probably be chosen for the stitching.

The linen square was then mounted onto another larger piece of linen which had been stretched across the linen-covered balsa wood subframe. This second piece of linen was different in colour, weave and texture but sympathetic to and enhancing the Coptic piece. A small square was cut out of both pieces of supporting linen, and a perspex-covered window was made in the hardboard backing to reveal a portion of the reverse side of the Coptic weaving which was of special interest. Finally, the whole was glazed and framed in the way we have already described. Nothing was added to the Coptic piece itself, nothing was taken away, but, by putting the piece on to the linen, it looked whole and pleasant.

Prince Rupert's coat
The next example of conservation technique concerns a garment. This was a coat, said to have been worn by Prince Rupert of the Rhine. When this beautiful parchment-coloured coat arrived for treatment it was, almost literally, in shreds. The material was woven with a silk warp and woollen weft. The silk warps had disintegrated to a very great extent, as can be seen in the photograph. Obviously the material would need support but this would mean getting it flat, in order to apply it to a supporting material in an embroidery frame. But material which has been

98 *Prince Rupert's coat before conservation.*

made into a garment has been cut and shaped and joined so that few parts of it remain quite flat. It would seem necessary, then, to undo seams to make the various parts of a garment flat enough for treatment. Here we come to another decision regarding the ethics of conservation: the original stitching and making up of an historic garment have a great deal of importance to those who study costume, and it is always desirable to avoid unpicking. In the case of Prince Rupert's coat, it was necessary to apply parts of the coat to the supporting fabric, and this was only possible by undoing the lining and the seams where the sleeves were set into the shoulders.

The material chosen for support was of man-made fibre in the identical colour of the coat and slightly lighter in weight and very strong. Polyester fabrics can be very useful as supporting materials, because they are stable and have good resistance to light and humidity. Another possible supporting material would have been silk crepeline, but in this case it was felt that it would not have been strong enough to give adequate support, nor heavy enough to give back the original weight to the whole garment.

Having chosen the supporting material, this was stretched into an embroidery frame and the various parts of the coat were laid on it in turn and applied to it by stitching, using a very fine needle and threads drawn from another piece of the supporting material. How this attaching was done is shown in the photograph. The broken threads of the silk were held in place with entomological pins and then stitched down using a pattern of couching – laying fine threads of the man-made fibre across the broken silk threads in long stitches, caught down by smaller stitches at regular intervals. The fine threads of the couching were invisible from even a short distance and the general improvement made by tidying the broken threads of the old material made the piece look whole again. The beautiful parchment lace decoration was vacuum cleaned and the garment reassembled.

99 *The coat on the support material in a large embroidery frame.*

100 *Part of Prince Rupert's coat during conservation treatment, being applied to supporting fabric with couching. Note entomological pins holding broken silk threads in position until the couching stitching can take over.*

One of the most important results of conserving textiles by stitching is that they still retain their essential qualities of moving and draping after treatment. This method of conservation can be successfully used on almost any fabric and is very suitable for brocade and damask, especially if the colours of the couching threads follow the colours of the pattern on the old material and are fine and unobtrusive. The supporting material must be chosen carefully, both for colour and weight, so that if there are any actual holes or missing areas in the old textile, the supporting fabric shows through and takes over to fill the gap. The casual observer is likely to accept the piece as being in a much better condition than it really is, but for the student who goes near to examine the piece really closely the conservation technique is soon revealed, and he can concentrate on his studies of the original textile. The conservation of Prince Rupert's coat was the work of an experienced professional conservator and took 500 hours, using a technique which required a high degree of consistency and application.

Very fine, thin fragile textiles can be given support by applying them to fine net or silk crepeline. Crepeline should always be washed before being used as a supporting material in order to remove the dressing used in its manufacture to give it body. The method of treatment is much the same as that used in the conservation of Prince Rupert's coat. The supporting material is framed up and the old textile laid on it and stitched with an appropriate thread wherever it needs support. When the pieces are removed from the frame, the net or crepeline can be cut away from the back of the old textile wherever it is not needed.

Doge's parasol

A rather similar method of supporting an old and fragile fabric using a stitching technique onto a supportive material was employed in the conservation of a beautiful and unusual parasol, said to have belonged to a Venetian doge at the end of the seventeenth century, and now at Waddesdon Manor, Buckinghamshire, which belongs to the National Trust. The outer cover

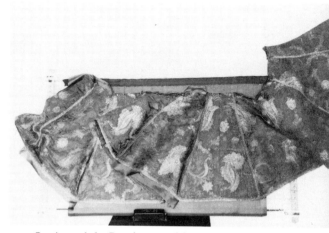

102 *Sections of the Doge's parasol in an embroidery frame, to be supported by couching onto red jap silk using a brick stitch method of couching.*

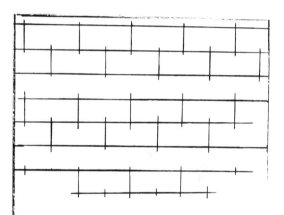

103 *Brick stitch method of couching.*

was of red silk brocaded in gold, and the lining was of fine grey-green taffeta which had probably been light blue when new, on which were painted gold stars. The cover, made up of ten triangular pieces, had been removed from the parasol frame in four pieces and washed before it came to us. Unfortunately, no record had been kept as to where each piece went, which made eventual reassembly very difficult and proved – if proof were needed – the wisdom of templates and marking and making copious notes whenever anything is taken apart, even if all the pieces appear to be interchangeable, as these did. They were, in fact, all slightly different, but had to go back in the right order, which was very difficult

104 *Close-up of part of a panel before treatment.*

to determine.

The four pieces were supported on monofilament screening and rewashed to straighten out the weft threads of the brocade which had become rather twisted. When dry the panels were stitched, section by section, to a support of red jap silk which was mounted in an embroidery frame. The gold braid outline of the gold brocade design was sewn down with polyester threads. Where the warp threads in the brocade were missing, couching threads of polyester were laid and sewn down. The stitches

105 *Close-up of panel after treatment.*

were made over two laid threads in a brick stitch fashion which broke up the shiny surface of the exposed weft threads, and did not pull them down, thus avoiding that quilted look which can occur when traditional couching methods are used. The silk lining was supported with resin-coated net and the top re-lined with white/cream jap silk, as the original lining had disintegrated round the edges where it was fixed to the frame. The gold fringe was straightened and cleaned.

Such a project as this should be attempted only by, or under the constant supervision of, a trained and experienced conservator.

Victorian parasol

We treated another parasol – this time a very pretty Victorian one belonging to the Exeter Museum – and in doing so evolved a method of preventing strain on parasols which have to remain open for any length of time, as would be the case if they were ever on exhibition. This one was pagoda-shaped, had eight whalebone spokes and a cover of pale green and yellow warp-printed taffeta with a yellow frill, all covered in black silk lace, and a long silk fringe

106 *The parasol conserved.*

107 *Line drawing to show method of relieving strain on parasol by attaching tape all round the edge.*

round the edge. The lining of the parasol was of white silk which had been subjected to so much strain, owing to the shape of the parasol, that it had split. The parasol was taken apart, cleaned, the damaged lining repaired and strengthened, and then the parasol was reassembled. It was the lining which gave the pagoda shape to the parasol and it seemed sensible to think of a method to relieve the very obvious strain on the lining panels so that they would not split again. The solution to the problem was found by fitting a narrow tape, stitching it to the end of each spoke so that it stretched all round the inside perimeter of the parasol. It was slightly tighter than the outside edge of the lining and could, therefore, take the strain. The drawing illustrates the position of the tape, which is very unobtrusive; if it is noticed, its purpose is so obvious that attention does not linger on it.

Quaker-dressed doll

The conservation of items of costume includes, of course, treatment of dolls and their clothing. Undressing an old doll should be done with care and notes should be taken of the order and way in which the clothes were put on the doll. Those who study the history of costume are always interested in clues which will help determine exactly how garments were worn, and some-

times the way a doll was dressed helps solve some of the puzzles which still remain.

One of the most interesting tasks we had in this area was the conservation of a doll dressed as a Quaker. It was difficult to date the doll exactly because, as a Quaker, one would not expect her to be dressed in the latest fashion of her time, but she was probably dressed at about the end of the eighteenth or beginning of the nineteenth century. All her clothes were dirty and worn but she had a wardrobe of several shawls, both muslin and silk, and two bonnets. All the white fabrics of the clothing could be washed. The white linen apron was very fragile indeed and needed the support of nylon net for washing. All the pieces washed successfully and dried straight and smooth and so did not require ironing.

The skirt of the doll's dress was of woven silk in a plain weave which originally would have made a fairly stiff fabric. Examination of a selvedge inside one seam showed which were warp and which weft threads, and we could see that the warp threads were less strong than the weft as the broken parts in the silk all lay in the same direction. It is possible that these warp threads had been given some treatment or dressing before weaving to prevent the silk fraying in the loom, and it was this which had eventually weakened the threads. When damage of this kind appears anywhere in a textile, it indicates the possibility that the rest of those threads (in this case, the warps) will be weak everywhere, even though they have not yet broken in other areas, and therefore all-over support is needed. After consideration the material of the skirt was detached so that it could be repaired by being supported on a fine polyester crepeline mounted in an embroidery frame and the broken silk was held in place by stitching with a fine silk thread dyed to match. The technique of support was very similar to that used for Prince Rupert's coat.

The bodice of the dress presented greater difficulties. Original stitching used in the making up of garments should be retained wherever possible, but as the bodice of this doll's dress was lined it would have had to be taken apart if it were to be treated in the same way as the

108–116 *Sequence showing redressing of a Quaker Doll.*

108 Doll and clothes before cleaning and conservation.

material of the skirt. Although repairing through lining is not usually to be recommended because it can make the fabric stiffer and clumsier than it ought to be, it was decided, because of the small size of the bodice and the importance of retaining the original stitching, that the lining should be used as the supporting material and no unpicking undertaken.

The doll had only one shoe, made from black satin-woven silk over white alum-treated leather. She wore white gloves, also of alum-treated leather; these were not removed as they were too brittle, and the only cleaning attempted on the shoe and gloves was a gentle dusting with a sable brush. Water would have removed the alum treatment had they been washed, and that would have just left old, untreated skin. Cleaning fluids would have made the leather more brittle. The missing shoe was replaced with one made up from black felt, simply for appearance's sake. Most of the other items of clothing were in fair condition and were replaced after cleaning.

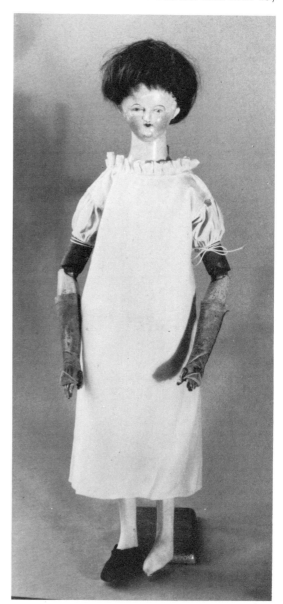

109 Doll cleaned.

110 Doll in basic undergarment.

111 Doll in corsets and underskirt with pockets and white half sleeves.

112 Doll with skirt, and pockets on the outside.

113 Top and skirt of dress on.

114 With bonnet and a fichu.

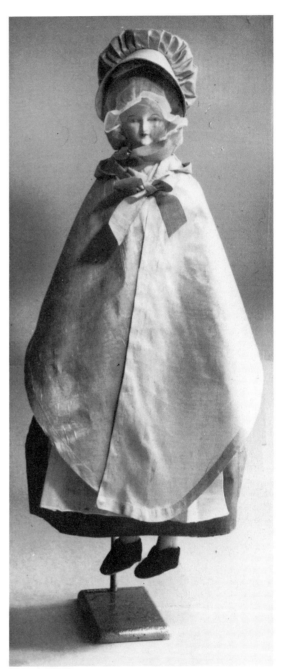

115 Changing to an outdoor bonnet, wearing a small shawl.

116 Another change to a longer wrap and another bonnet.

Two altar frontals

An altar frontal dated about 1910 was sent to us for conservation. It was of silk damask with silk and jap gold embroidery. There was considerable damage, from rubbing, to the top of the frontal and some of the silk damask had worn right through. The frontal was first vacuum-cleaned through screening and then taken apart. There had been some previous repairing done by stitching through to the material backing the embroidery and some of these repairing stitches were removed. When the piece was apart, it could be seen that some extra of the original damask had been folded back round the edges when the piece had been made up, and that the embroidery had been correctly done through the damask supported by a backing material. The damask and supporting material, now as one, were put into an embroidery frame, and pieces of this extra damask were cut off and put between the damaged damask and the backing, in such a way that the pattern of the damask was matched in these patches. The pieces were held in position with a couching method of stitching and the repairs effected so that the top of the damask looked whole again. When all the damaged areas had been treated, the frontal was reassembled.

The second altar frontal had very heavy gold embroidery on a thin silk fabric, but this work had been done without the support of a backing material. When new the frontal must have looked very lovely and had obviously been the result of a great many hours of work but, because the background material was so thin and had been called upon to take the considerable weight of the gold embroidery, it had disintegrated to the point where it could no longer give support. Supporting the original embroidery on a new material matching in colour and design, suitably backed with a firm linen support, would have been the only way to save even part of the frontal, and this would have been a very lengthy process, expensive beyond the value of the piece. Weighty embroidery, particularly if metal threads are used, should be really well supported not only by materials on which the work is done, but also with an

117 *Altar frontal.*

118 *Detail of altar frontal.*

adequate backing to that material. Had this frontal been properly supported by a backing in the first place, even the rather thin material chosen would have survived much longer than it did.

An incomplete costume

To make an object comprehensible in display, it might be necessary to add the semblance of a missing part. We can quote the case of the nineteenth-century dress acquired by a collector and brought for treatment. The dress material had come from India and was decorated

119 *Incomplete dress, decorated with beetle wings. Front view, after having been given sleeves.*

with a design made up of beetle wings. These green, iridescent, sequin-like wings gave a most unusual and attractive appearance to the material. The dress, unfortunately, had no sleeves, and in its incomplete state meant very little to anyone.

Research was done to find what sort of sleeves a dress of that style and date would have had, and a possible sleeve pattern was established. New sleeves were then made, using a modern fabric as nearly matching the original material of the dress as possible. Our collection of potentially useful items yielded just enough similar beetle wings to decorate the edges of the new sleeves. To the casual observer the dress would seem to be an authentic example of its period. A serious student of costume, however, while agreeing, or possibly disagreeing, with the style of the new sleeves for the dress, would see at once on close examination that they were not original. The addition of the new sleeves made the dress understandable for display but no attempt had been made to deceive. The material of the main part of the dress provided a good example of the method of using beetle wings as a decoration and, as such, deserved to be seen.

Tapestry and canvas-work

Woven tapestry is often used as an upholstery material and may need restoration so that it can continue to be used. Even more common is the canvas-work embroidery which is frequently called tapestry. This description has almost become accepted as correct in Britain, where noblewomen were never associated with weaving on a loom as they were in some other parts of the world, such as Germany and Scandinavia. From Tudor times, British needleworkers have imitated woven tapestries by embroidering on canvas, and their work has become known as tapestry work or, simply, tapestry. In America it is called needlepoint, possibly because *gros-point* and *petit-point* are the two most commonly used canvas-work stitches.

It is essential to know the difference between tapestry and canvas-work, and how each was produced, if one is going to do any conservation or restoration on either of them. Tapestry has been woven on a loom using a plain weave in which the warp threads are closely covered by the weft threads. Canvas-work, on the other hand, is embroidery done with a needle and threads of wool or silk on an existing base of canvas.

The replacement of missing stitches in canvas work or the restoration of fragile areas in woven tapestry should always be done onto a supporting fabric. We use linen scrim, the material used for cleaning windows, as a supporting material for canvas-work, and for tapestry we use scrim, linen crash or brown holland, which is also used for linings. These materials need to be allowed to shrink before use, however small the pieces are; if they shrink later they could cause strain and pull on the textile they are supporting. Our method of shrinking has been described in Chapter 7. If the material is kept smooth throughout the process, no ironing will be needed. The amount of shrinkage will vary, but before and after measurements will always prove the wisdom of shrinking before use. Remember, a damp atmosphere could cause problems later.

The next stage is to frame up the supporting material. The frame must be large enough to take a piece of linen or scrim which will allow a border of at least 2 in (5 cm) all round the textile to be treated. The upholsterer will be glad of this border to pull on when returning the restored textile cover to its piece of furniture. Sew the ends of the linen or scrim firmly to the webbing on the frame rollers and roll the material evenly up from one end until there is a reasonable area on which to work. Put stretchers into the sides of the frame giving the framed support material an even but slightly slack tension. As stitching is done through both the supporting and the old textile, the respective tensions are important. The old textile should be comfortably stretched and taut during treatment, but if the supporting material is too tight, it will pull and distort the old textile. On the other hand, if it is too loose, it will not give adequate support. If, despite all your care, there is a tight area, once restoration

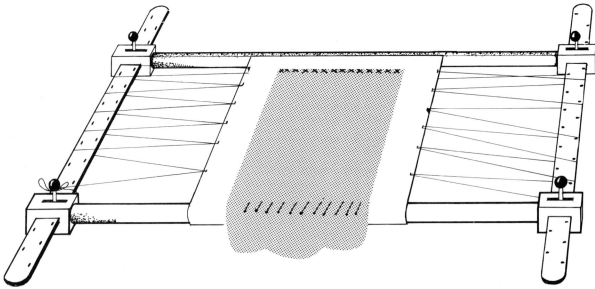

120 *Piece framed up for conservation/restoration. It is stitched to the backing material at the end from which work is done, but the piece is longer and therefore has to be pinned at the other side of the frame; the work is rolled towards the worker as the stitching is done. The frame has to be undone at the sides each time the work is rolled and the frame refixed to the correct tension.*

of the piece is finished and it is removed from the frame it is possible to relieve the tension by slitting the supporting fabric where no stitches come through. Quite a small slit will make a great difference.

Once the supporting material is in the frame correctly, first pin and then, using linen thread, stitch the bottom edge of the old textile to it at one end about 3 in (8 cm) up from the webbing. If the piece to be treated is canvas-work, place it so that the design is the right way round and work from the bottom upwards. If the piece is tapestry, however, it is essential to see that the warp threads run from the bottom to the top of the frame, parallel with the side stretchers.

Having secured the bottom edge of the piece to the supporting material in the frame, pull the tapestry or canvas-work gently but firmly up to the top roller and pin it in place to the extra supporting material. Use strong pins and continue to pin and adjust until the old fabric is

evenly stretched. Both the warp threads of tapestry and canvas threads are usually quite strong, so no damage should occur providing care is taken and adjustments are made gradually. The rest of the old textile will hang down behind the frame. Once the tensions of the old and the supporting materials are correct, put the side tapes on to keep the old textile quite straight. Before beginning any stitching, check once more that the supporting material is slightly loose underneath the smoothly-stretched old textile.

Obviously, once the area stretched in the frame has been repaired the frame will be undone, the treated portion will be rolled on to the bottom roller, another area of supporting material unrolled from the top roller and another portion of the old textile stretched for treatment. If the piece of old textile is small enough to go on the frame as a whole, make sure that the supporting material is slightly loose before beginning work.

For the actual stitching, use wool to replace wool and a tapestry needle of a size to suit the thickness of the thread. We recommend Appleton's crewel wool; the individual strands are fine, but any number can be used together to make up the exact thickness required. There is a great range of colour available and, if necessary, strands of different colours can be used together to achieve an elusive shade. Make a knot at the end of the repairing thread. Take the needle through the right side at a point 3–4 in (8–10 cm) away from the area to be treated and leave the knot on top of the *right* side of the work, to be cut off later. When the necessary stitching has been completed, finish off by bringing the needle through to the right side at a point about 3 in (8 cm) from the treated area and leave a length of unused thread to be cut off later. Knots should never be left on the wrong side, especially in material used as upholstery, as they will cause damage. We have seen knots left on the back of canvas-work which have actually worn holes in canvas and embroidery and have worked their way through to the right side.

Repairing tapestries

If tapestry is being repaired remember that the piece was originally woven on a loom and, therefore, a weaving technique of inserting the needle under one warp thread and over the next must be used when replacing missing weft threads. Never make a stitch which goes through a warp thread as this could cause strain later and would, in any case, have been impossible during the original weaving of the tapestry. A stitch through weft threads is undesirable but

not so serious. Take all stitches through both the old textile and the supporting fabric. It is when one begins to repair woven tapestry that one realises how necessary it is to understand how a piece was made in the first place if one is to achieve success in conservation or restoration.

Silk areas are treated by couching down all weak parts with stranded cotton in unobtrusive shades. We do not attempt any reweaving of silk. Any restoration work, however invisible and unobtrusive it is when done, is likely to become somewhat obvious as time passes, because the colours of new fibres used will themselves change, and a perfect match of colour at the time of restoration may eventually fade to something completely different, as colour plate 1 showed. If silk areas are rewoven, this fact can become very obvious after a short time.

The highlights, around flowers for instance, can be successfully repaired by using Clark's Anchor stranded cotton. In the chair cover of a fine Soho tapestry, illustrated here, which

121 *Chair seat on linen in frame. Warps go away from the conservator as this is tapestry. The piece is pinned before being sewn to the backing at the nearest end.*

122 *Soho tapestry chair cover after conservation.*

comes from Uppark in Sussex and belongs to the National Trust, there was a blue sky area woven in silk which had almost disappeared. The conservation was effected by using a supporting material of a blue cotton poplin. The warp threads of the tapestry were sound and intact and these (using blue embroidery cotton) were couched down straight and even onto the blue supporting material. Small traces of the original silk weft were incorporated, wherever they had remained, by being caught with the couching stitching. The visual result, even from a short distance, is of a complete sky area and, as there is so little that is new material, it is hoped that the appearance of the piece will remain unaltered for a very long time without the conservation/restoration becoming too obvious. After the work was removed from the frame, the parts of the blue supporting material which had not been stitched into were cut away so that there would be no chance of their pulling or

123 *The upholstery was conserved by couching the blue silk sky area onto blue supporting material, the rest of the seat being supported similarly in appropriate colours – before conservation.*

distorting the tapestry above. This was necessary as the technique used had meant that the supporting material had not been allowed to be loose under the old textile.

In most pieces of tapestry used as upholstery the warps remain fairly strong even if the weft threads have deteriorated, but sometimes warps

have been cut or broken and it is necessary to replace these before anything can be done to replace the weft. To replace a warp choose a thread slightly thinner than the existing warp, and of strong cotton if proper woollen warp thread is not available. There is a kind of cotton fishing line which is very suitable, or fine cotton crochet or macramé thread could be used. Thread a length of this warp substitute into a tapestry needle and knot the end. Put the needle into the right side of the tapestry about 3 in (8 cm) below the broken warp end and draw it

124 *Broken warps on edge of tapestry chair seat made safe by continuing linen support to fill in a missing area (right side).*

through until the knot lies on the surface. It can be cut off later. Bring the needle to the surface of the tapestry again between two warp threads and about $\frac{1}{2}$ in (13 mm) below the broken warp end. Now insert the point of the needle into the weft and run it under the weft threads along the path of the broken warp thread until it appears at the place that the warp is broken. Grip the point end of the needle with pliers. Draw the needle, followed by the replacement warp, through gently. Next insert the point of the needle beside the place where the other end of the broken warp appears and run it through the weft alongside the old warp, bringing it out at the back of the tapestry about 1 in (2.5 cm) away from the break. Again pull the needle and following thread through with pliers. Draw the replacement warp through until it is firm and its tension is the same as the other warp threads. Take a stitch over an existing warp thread on the back of the tapestry to fasten it in place. If several warp threads have to be replaced next to each other, make new warps in the same way but vary the points at which you insert the needle, either making them nearer or further away from the breaks in the warps, so that the double thickness of warps does not become obvious. Always be careful to pull or push the needle exactly in line with the existing warps so that there is as little damage to the surrounding weft as possible, as the whole area could well be very fragile. Be especially careful to replace the warps correctly so that the broken ends which you join really do belong to the same original warp. If this is not done there might be an odd end at one side of a

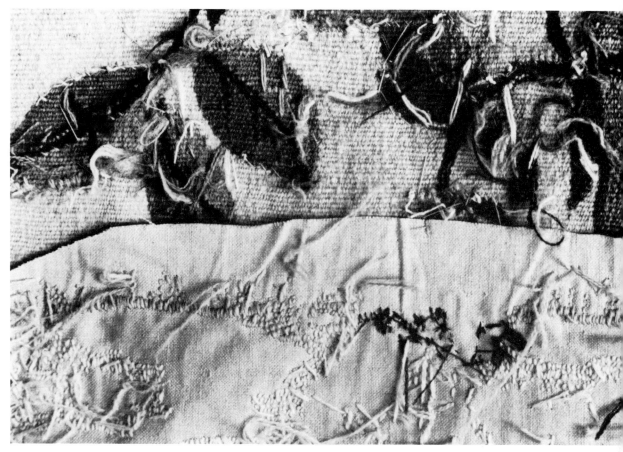

125 *Linen support on tapestry chair seat. Reverse side of figure 124.*

hole, and any subsequent reweaving will not be straight and will be visually disturbing. If there is a missing area at the edge of a piece, as could well happen on the cover taken from a piece of furniture, then make new warps stretching from the tapestry and anchor them to the linen supporting fabric at the other end. Sew down any short broken warp ends on to the linen and repair over these to cover them and supply the missing area of tapestry.

Repairing canvas-work

Canvas-work embroidery covers for chair seats, backs and arms, and for stool tops, are probably the most usual of all upholstery covers which might be restored at home. Having removed the pieces, made templates of them, and washed and dried them in shape, the amount of repair needed can then be seen. Frame up washed scrim in the way described for framing linen used to support tapestry. (p. 113).

Scrim is strong and open in weave and very suitable for supporting canvas-work. If the canvas is still strong, the replacement of missing embroidery may be all the restoration that is needed and it might be possible to do this without using scrim as support. It is advisable, however, to do the work in a frame rather than in the hand, because the stretching back into shape that would almost certainly be necessary after working in the hand could cause damage. Canvas-work done in a frame requires little or no stretching when finished, and the less strain on the canvas the better.

If there are one or two strands of the canvas missing it is possible to embroider straight through to the scrim to replace the stitches;

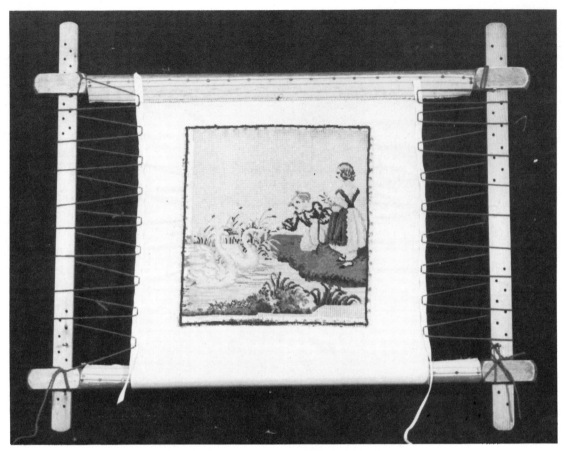

126 Canvas-work panel from screen – applied to framed support material for stitching – seen from the front.

better still, first replace the missing threads of canvas with linen thread, rather in the way one can replace missing warp threads in tapestry, except that the missing canvas threads may need to be replaced both horizontally and vertically. This is best done by stitching through the supporting scrim after the work is framed up. If, however, there is an actual hole, a patch of canvas may be needed. This must be exactly the same grade as the original canvas and should be stitched in place on the wrong side of the embroidery, exactly matching the threads in each direction, before the work is put in a frame. This is very difficult to do without making a bulky area around the patch because of the two thicknesses of canvas and should be avoided if

any other way of replacing the missing area can be found.

The technique of repairing canvas-work is almost identical to that of doing the embroidery in the first place. Using a tapestry needle, replace wool with wool, silk with silk if available or use embroidery cotton, and replace bead work with wool or silk unless there are old beads available. Again, we recommend Appleton's crewel wool and DMC or Anchor stranded cotton. It is necessary to use exactly the same canvas-work stitches as in the original, but it is often only necessary to replace the top stitch in cross stitch, where the old one has become worn or broken. A few stitches in a weak area will make it safe and will attach the old textile to the supporting scrim material – which, again, must always be slightly loose.

Be prepared for all sorts of odd stitching in the original and fall in with them, whatever private

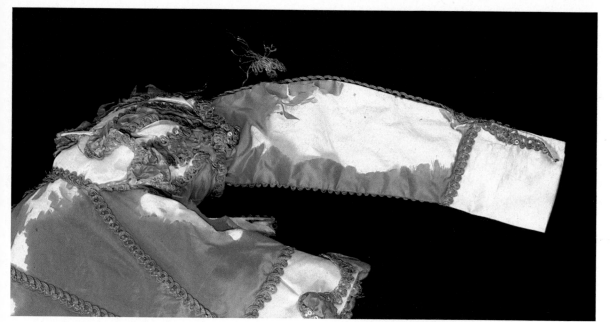

6 Above *Page of honour costume worn by Charles Bagot at the coronation of King George IV. The photograph shows a detail of the doublet sleeve before conservation.*

7 *The doublet after conservation. Specially dyed silk was inset behind the damaged portion. The entire page's costume is on display at Levens Hall, Kendall.*

8 *Guidon of the 10th Light Dragoons. Detail before conservation showing damage by fire and staining by water.*

9 *After conservation showing patches behind damaged areas.*

10 *Entire guidon after conservation.*

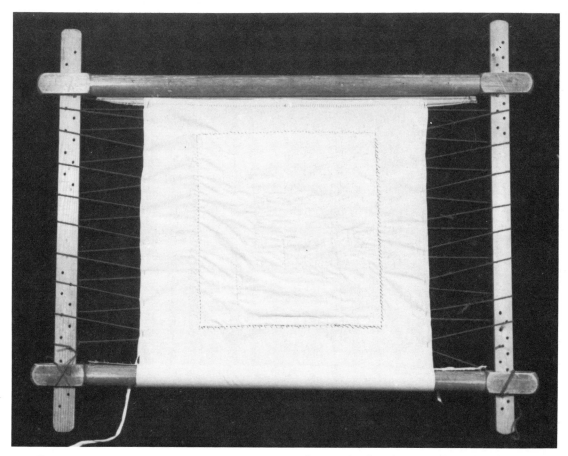

127 Reverse side of canvas-work picture. The stitching has been done in a neutral shade, and the picture attached to the support with as few stitches as were necessary to provide proper support and secure loose threads. The backing material, although loose so as not to exert any pull or drag, provides adequate support for the picture, which remains quite flat and tidy.

thoughts you may have about the technique of the person who did the embroidery in the first place. It is surprising what a lot one can learn about the person who did the original work. In embroidery repair, particularly, one comes into personal contact with the past. We once had to restore two canvas-work chair seats from the same source. Working on them we eventually realised that they had actually started out as identically designed pieces, but the treatment of each had been so different that they had at first seemed completely unrelated, not only in tech-

nique and colour but even in design. We felt that they must have been the work of two very different members of the same household. Each was restored and each, happily, retained its character.

Gold work

Many people possess examples of oriental embroidery with gold work. These pieces may be displayed as hangings or on screens, and they become very obviously in need of attention if the gold threads become loose. The design is lost in a tangled jumble of thin gold threads which present a rather daunting challenge.

First, examine the piece carefully and, if the design can be discerned, possibly in the form of stitch holes, and if the gold threads merely seem loose rather than actually missing, then the problem of making the piece look right again

128 *Piece of canvas-work before conservation. Former unsuitable repairs and actual holes were dealt with by unpicking, backing the whole piece with linen and stitching where necessary.*

129 *The picture conserved and in a sub-frame. An elopement, a fire, a burglary, a possible drowning and a kill by a dog explain the despair shown by the central figure, and the name 'Disasters', which the piece acquired while undergoing conservation.*

may be one of patience rather than any complicated technique. If the piece is lined, remove the lining, marking the top for its correct replacement later. If the background material on which the embroidery has been worked is in good condition, clean with a vacuum cleaner and screening, and put the piece into an embroidery frame. If the background material seems fragile or has any weak areas clean it carefully, then select a suitable supporting material, such as a piece of washed lightweight cotton in a matching colour, frame it up and apply the embroidered material to it. If the piece is too long for convenient working use the method described earlier for applying long pieces of tapestry or canvas-work to a backing material in a frame (p. 114).

Once the piece is in the frame, whether supported by a backing material or not, it will be possible to catch down the loose gold threads. It will generally be found that any embroidery done in silk will have kept well and be intact, but the gold threads used in the embroidery will have been caught down with couching stitches which are often of a thin, soft thread which does not wear well. When these threads break they cause the escape of the gold threads which, released from their whorls and spirals, seem to spring in all directions. Find a place where the gold is still attached, look for the stitch holes nearby and work from there to restore the pattern of the gold threads. Entomological pins are a great help in anchoring springy pieces of gold embroidery thread until the proper place can be found. Try to make replacement stitches into the original needle holes and choose a thread to match, in colour and thickness, the remaining couching threads. The infuriating thing is to end up with some gold for which there seems no place, which possibly means that a whorl or circle has been left out in the repairing, so pin first and try to fit in all the loose gold threads.

With patience, this is not particularly difficult conservation work, and the results are very rewarding as the picture becomes tidy and the design clear again. Tension is important both in the stitching and between embroidery and supporting material, if that is used. If the background requires some stitching by way of repair, do this as unobtrusively as possible, perhaps near or into the embroidery, or in a way similar to the other examples we have given for supporting a fragile fabric on to a new piece when working in a frame.

Patchwork

The compatibility of different fibres and fabrics should be considered if they are to be put together in the same object. Almost all of us have seen what can happen when fabrics, not only of different fibres but also of different degrees of wear and age, are put together in a patchwork quilt. After a few years the patches of old material, especially of silk, disintegrate, while patches of new material or longer lasting cotton and linen remain intact and strong. If silk is used in patchwork quilts it is best if all the patches are of silk, and great care should be given to the quilt from the outset.

Protection can be given to those parts of an old patchwork quilt which have become split or have perished by stitching pieces of fine net or washed crepeline in appropriate colours over the damaged areas. It should be possible to make the stitches necessary to attach the net or crepeline into the original stitching at the edges of the patches. Do not take the stitches through to the lining as this could cause strain. Net and crepeline can be dyed if it is not possible to buy the right colour, but they are both almost transparent, so finding the colour that makes them almost invisible is no great problem. This method of applying net or crepeline to keep fragile and loose fibres in place and keep them safe can be used in cases where old fabrics need such protection, but these textiles must, of course, always be treated with great care and handled as little as possible.

Conclusions

All the treatments we have described for conservation or restoration involve sewing. Needles do, of course, make holes but careful stitching –

always inserting the needle between, and not into, the threads of the material – is potentially the least damaging form of treatment and does have the great advantage that it is reversible now and in the future. There are other techniques used by trained professionals but we feel that descriptions of these techniques would be beyond the scope of this book.

Up to now the book has been chiefly concerned with the care of old textile objects, but many people who find textiles interesting are also involved with the making up of new materials, whether in weaving, embroidery, dressmaking or plain sewing. Some of the work now being done will certainly be treasured in the future as examples of our own time, either for artistic or historic merit. Few people set out deliberately to produce masterpieces, but we have described how many and varied are the causes of deterioration in textiles, and anyone working with them would be well advised to give some thought to the suitability and lasting qualities of the materials they used before spending hours in skilful work on an object which, by the nature of its compound materials, cannot survive for any length of time.

Even beautifully designed and executed pieces can deteriorate in a relatively short period if the original materials are of poor quality, are incompatible with one another, or have been put under stress or strain and not given adequate support. Much embroidery and similar work is, of course, done as a hobby or on a voluntary basis – a labour of love – but if one costs out the hours that are spent, one realises how penny-wise, pound-foolish it is to use inferior or unsuitable materials for the time and talent involved.

The time to make all decisions of this kind is, obviously, before starting the work. As with conservation, so with new work: think ahead and try to anticipate where trouble could arise and then prevent it happening. If this becomes an attitude of mind, it is really very easy. Anyone who cares for the textile arts and who plays even a small part in preserving our heritage, both of objects and skills, will continue to experience very real satisfaction.

9

Equipment and information

With all appliances and means to boot.
Shakespeare, *Henry IV*

Tools

In any undertaking, having the right tools and equipment makes for efficiency and involves the operator in the least effort. For anyone undertaking textile conservation, these are usually acquired in three ways.

Firstly, there are those aids which one would normally find in the possession of any person who has dealt with textiles and is used to handling them, whether in ordinary household sewing, in embroidery, dressmaking or other creative skills. These tools would include scissors, needles, threads, thimbles, an iron and possibly equipment for special interests – embroidery frames, sewing machine, dressmaker's dummy, etc.

Secondly, if any conservation work is to be done, there would be additional items which would have to be acquired as they were needed. Such pieces of equipment might well include a special vessel for washing fragile fabrics, a piece of softboard and some melinex film and brass pins for drying correctly, monofilament screening (filtration fabric) and one or more embroidery frames, together with specialised small items such as tweezers, a magnifying glass and a much wider selection of needles, threads and wools than would be found in a normal household.

Thirdly, there is the sort of equipment which a much more experienced conservator or a group working together would hope to own for efficient working. Here one would expect to find

some trestle supports for embroidery frames, a large table or table tops which could be used with the trestles, larger washing vessels, a supply of nets, dyes and dyeing vessels, stocks of supporting materials, threads, embroidery cottons and wools, large pieces of softboard, rolls of melinex and monofilament screening and so on.

One builds up stock and equipment as they are needed, and we have tried to make out a reasonably comprehensive list to include most of the items in the above three categories. However, no list of equipment can be complete for the simple reason that, as each textile object presents its own problem in conservation, the solving of that problem may require something which has to be bought – or borrowed – for that special treatment. In the early stages one can improvise, but there comes a point when only the correct piece of equipment will do. Once it has been acquired, however, it can be used again and again in other situations.

The acquisition of tools for conservation can become almost an attitude of mind. The serious conservator will make a habit of collecting catalogues, not only from the more obvious places like embroidery suppliers, but also from craft shops of every kind, surgical instrument makers (nurses' scissors are very sharp and a useful shape; medical tweezers are very fine and sharp for unpicking; surgeons' needles are invaluable at times because they are curved and angled), and art supply shops (artists' brushes have long, gentle bristles). A true conservator never passes a display of tools, no matter for

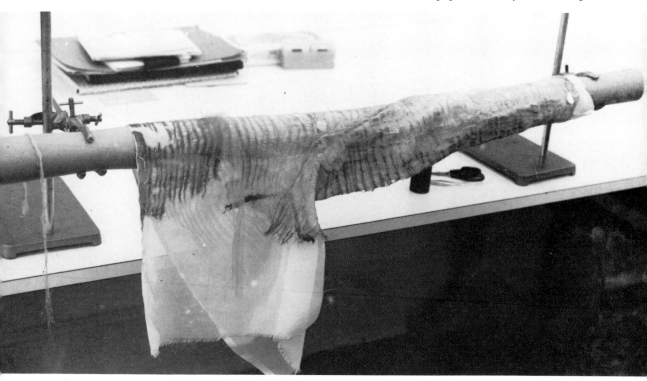

130 *Ingenuity will often provide suitable equipment. In this case, the problem was to apply supporting material by a stitching method to the delicate fabric of a sleeve without undoing the seam.*

what trade or profession it is intended, without looking to see if there is something there which would be of use. In this way, one always knows just where to buy the right tools for a particular job if the occasion arises. The list we have given is one which we feel would supply the requirements for a great deal of work. All the items are proven in use but more could be added as required and, of course, all are not essential in the early stages of conservation work or for someone who simply wants to do a little conserving or restoring to keep a few treasured textiles safe.

Equipment

Removal of surface dust

Vacuum cleaner – must have hand-held dusting attachment and preferably choice of suction strength.

Monofilament screening (filtration fabric) in several sizes (minimum one square yard/metre) with either bound edges or framed with battens.

To clean glass in frames or display cabinets – wash leather or soft cloths wrung out in water to which an anti-static liquid (such as Comfort or Softrinse) has been added, or Perspex No. 3 Polish – also an anti-static.

Sable paint brush – for very light removal of dust from crevices.

Washing

Washing vessels for small items – shallow, flat-bottomed, in various sizes. Photographers' developing trays are very suitable.

Or a purpose-built washing table – made of stainless steel or other non-reactive material with drainage outlet.

Or a large sheet of heavy-duty polythene, assorted bricks, wood, etc. – for emergency outside washing tank.

Or a sunken bath. The Textile Conservation

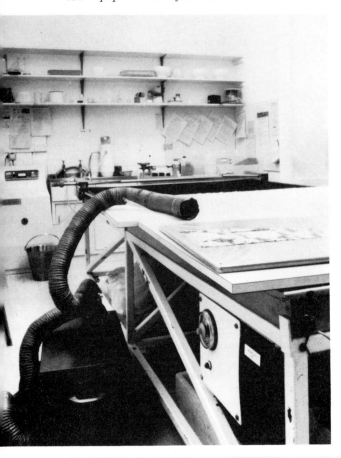

131 *Washing table, here supporting table tops on which small textiles are drying flat on melinex-covered softboard. Along the back wall can be seen the de-ionising unit, sink, work top holding portable Permutit water softener, scales and other equipment. The de-humidifying hose is drawing damp air from the washed textiles for dispersal via the other hose through the open window.*

Centre is fortunate to have an indoor, purpose-built, sunken tiled bath, with drainage, for washing large textiles.

Supply of softened water – ideally obtained through a Permutit water softener or a de-ioniser. Alternatively, obtained by treating tap water with a softening agent. Soft water should always be used for both washing and intensive rinsing, with a final rinsing using distilled or de-ionised water.

Washing agents – Synperonic, Vulpex or Saponaria.

Sponges – artificial ones are quite satisfactory.

Monofilament screening and net for supporting during washing.

Softboard

Melinex film or polythene sheeting.

Brass pins.

132 *Water installations for the tiled tapestry-washing room.*

133 *Trestle.*

134 *Trestles supporting melamine-covered table tops.*

Conservation

Embroidery frames of assorted sizes; if only one is acquired then choose one with a 40 in (100 cm) tape.

Smaller frames with linen centres to which work can be quickly attached for treatment to small areas.

Trestles to support embroidery frames and/ or table tops.

At the Textile Conservation Centre we have a system whereby embroidery frames or specially made table tops can be supported by trestles. The table tops are covered on all sides and edges with white melamine. The tops are 6 ft (180 cm) long and 3 ft (90 cm) wide and, as they are exactly twice as long as they are wide, they can be put together on a module system, supported by trestles, to form the required size of table needed when lining tapestries or for dealing with very large textiles which have to be laid flat for examination or treatment.

The Textile Conservation Centre has had a special tapestry conservation frame made with three rollers – two carry the actual tapestry undergoing treatment and the third holds the supporting scrim through which stitches are made and which supplies support for the tapestry. The scrim is gradually unrolled as the work progresses and its support is needed. (Details of

135 *View of tapestry frame in use. Strip lighting fitted with Philips 47 fluorescent tubes. Note adjustable chair in the background.*

both the trestles and this special tapestry frame are available on request from the Centre.)

Materials

Monofilament screening (filtration fabric).
Melinex and polythene sheeting.
Fine nylon net.
Silk and polyester crepeline.
Linen for lining hangings, especially tapestries.
Scrim.
Linen thread which can be dyed if necessary.
Anchor stranded cotton in various colours.
DMC embroidery cotton in various colours.
Appleton's crewel wool in various colours.
Material for supporting old textiles is bought as needed.
Scissors – of various kinds for different needs.
Pins – glass-headed steel pins; brass lace pins; entomological pins.
Needles – in assorted sizes: crewel; tapestry; sharps; curved; etc.
Thimbles – assorted sizes.
Tweezers – assorted sizes.
Magnifying glass.
Measuring tapes and sticks – assorted sizes.
Sewing machine.
Acid-free tissue paper.
Lightweight iron, ironing board and sleeve board.
Pliers and other small tools.
Hardboard.
Storage boxes.
Polyvinyl acetate adhesive.
Small tag labels.
Dust sheets to cover work.
Polystyrene to make dummies and muslin to cover.
Dyestuffs as required.

Documentation

Camera capable of taking close-ups for detail.
Notebooks with pages for drawings.
Pencils for use near work. (Ballpoint pens can cause irremovable marks).

The workroom

There is another aspect of conservation work which should be included here, and that is the place of work – whether it is arranged as required, is a permanent location in a private house or a workroom shared by a group, possibly volunteers. No one can work well unless comfortable; therefore warm but well-ventilated conditions with good daylight, preferably from the north, should be the aim. Ordinary electric light distorts colours but a large workroom could be fitted with Philips 47 fluorescent tubes and then work can continue most of the year. (These tubes emit a light which has a colour mix which is the nearest artificial light to daylight.) Philips also make a good blue daylight bulb which is an enormous help for individuals working with a small adjustable angle lamp. A blue 60 watt bulb will be found to give sufficient light and true colour quality. It is also a great help against dazzle when working with gold thread, even in daylight.

Chairs should be comfortable. An adjustable typist's chair which enables a worker to turn round without getting up to reach for more thread, wool, etc. is a time and energy saver. Tables and embroidery frames should be at a comfortable height for working and should stand firm and steady. Embroidery frames are best supported on trestles because these can be adjusted to allow the frame to be at the most convenient height and angle. If trestles are not available, the ends of the frame should be rested on something firm and solid; it is impossible to do good work on an unsteady frame. Always keep work in a frame covered with a dust sheet, except when actually working – even then it pays to cover all the framed textile except the area actually under treatment. Be especially careful always to cover finished work which has been rolled round the end of the frame nearest to the operator, so that it cannot be rubbed by the worker's arms while sitting at the frame. If the frame has to be put away between work sessions, pin a dust sheet right round it so that it remains clean and safe while not being used. Never put

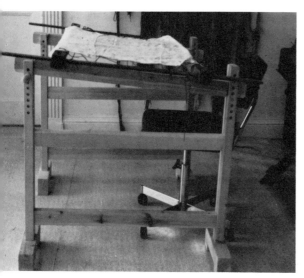

136 *Trestle supporting embroidery at an angle for comfortable working, using the adjustable chair. As no work is in progress the textile in the frame is covered.*

anything weighty on top of material in a frame as this can alter the tension of the framed fabric and the old fibres may not be sufficiently elastic to recover when the weight is removed.

If an iron has to be used, it should be a lightweight one. Set it at cool, but do not trust a thermostat completely and always test the heat before allowing the iron to touch an old fabric. Never leave an iron switched on and then go back to it expecting that heat will not have built up – it almost invariably does; irons left switched on are also a danger in every way and in all situations, not only when dealing with old fabrics. If the sole of the iron needs cleaning this can be done with candlewax, rubbed on the sole of the iron while it is warm (but switched off) and then rubbed off with a clean cloth. Never use anything harsh. Saucepan scourers or pads

of the wire-wool type will make the sole look clean but they leave tiny sharp particles behind to rust which can cause damage to fibres later.

The Textile Conservation Centre also has a laboratory for testing and research, and a dye room where materials used in support of fragile textiles in conservation are dyed to a shade most suitable to achieve the enhancement and understanding of the piece.

The conservator

No chapter on equipment would be complete without some reference to the one item without which no work is done: the conservator. All the processes need thought and take time, sometimes a very great deal of time, and a too-hurried decision or action can result in disaster, so no jobs should be undertaken by someone impatient who wants quick results.

Some of the sewing methods used to give overall support to very fragile fabrics can take a very long time to complete, and it is worth watching oneself to find out the length of time one can maintain a really high standard of work at any single session. This varies from person to person or even, in the same person, is dependent on how one feels. Try to learn to stop just short of one's optimum time of good work so that all important work is done at the best of one's ability. Be warned, however: conservation work is very more-ish, and there is often the temptation to go on for just a little longer. Being tired can cause mistakes. Stitching is a reversible process, but it is an unhappy way to prove it by having to unpick sub-standard or unacceptable work – far better to leave a piece of work which demands intense concentration until one is fresh enough to go on rather than push oneself when tired.

Appendix

Glossary

Alum – mineral salt used in treating animal skin and as a mordant in dyeing.

Applied – laid on and secured with stitching.

Appliqué – technique of applying decorative shapes by stitching.

Basic weaves –

   Plain weave – simple weave in which each weft thread goes under and over each warp thread in turn.

   Twill weave – weave in which weft threads go over two or more warp threads and under one or more in one row, progressing along by one or more in consecutive rows, thus producing a diagonal ribbed effect.

   Satin weave – weaving in which weft threads are allowed to float over several warp threads to achieve a shiny surface.

Batten – a strip of wood.

Bleeding – transference of colour from one area to an adjoining one by dye dissolving in moisture.

Brocade – weaving in which a design is achieved by using different coloured weft threads independent of the ground weave.

Bump – soft, thick cotton underlining.

Coptic – early Egyptian Christian.

Couching – technique of laying threads on the surface of a fabric and holding them in place by stitching across them at regular intervals.

Crewel needle – needle with a large eye and a sharp point.

Damask – fabric in an all-over colour in which a pattern is produced by the weaving technique used.

Felt – fibres matted together to form a fabric.

Gimp – form of braid used as a decorative edging, particularly in upholstery.

Gros point – large slanting stitch in canvas-work.

Jap silk – type of lightweight silk.

Petit point – small slanting stitch over one thread in canvas-work.

Raised work – embroidery which is padded or raised above the surface of the background, an example of which is stump work, usually executed on a satin ground and much used in the Stuart period to cover boxes or as pictures. Scenes, frequently Biblical in theme, show animals and figures, padded and moulded in the half-round or even separately modelled and then attached. Costumes, usually of the Stuart period, are of rich materials, often with sequins and pearls as decoration.

Sharps – normal sewing needles with small eyes and sharp points.

Stretcher – (1) wooden rectangular frame over which material, such as canvas for painting, is stretched; (2) removable side pieces of an embroidery frame.

Tapestry needles – needles with large eyes and blunt ends.

Template – cardboard or paper pattern made by drawing round the outer edge of an object.

Tent stitch – simple slanting stitch used in canvas-work. Also known as *gros point*, *petit point* and needlepoint.

Warp – threads, set up in a loom, running lengthwise, on which the weaving is done.

Weft – threads going under and over the warp threads from side to side in weaving.

Societies: U.K.

We invited various societies to provide notes of introduction to readers who might wish to make contact with them either with a view to membership to further special interests or to obtain some specialised information regarding textiles in their possession or care. All the groups we contacted cater for both active and less active members at many levels.

The inclusion of stamps (or, where applicable, international postal coupons) is always appreciated when a reply is requested from any society contacted.

The Association of Guilds of Weavers, Spinners and Dyers

Founded in 1955 as the successor of the pre-war organisation, it is the co-ordinating body of some 70 Guilds of Weavers, Spinners and Dyers throughout Britain.

The aims of the Association are to encourage and maintain integrity and excellence of craftsmanship in hand weaving, spinning and dyeing, to foster a sense of beauty of material, texture, colour and design, to provide opportunities for the interchange of information, for enlarging knowledge at holiday schools, exhibitions, lectures and library facilities and to co-operate with other bodies having like aims.

The individual affiliated Guilds are responsible for the running of their own affairs and the decision to affiliate to the Association is taken at local level. Once affiliated, however, they have a say in the running of the Association.

The Weavers' Journal, the publication of the Association which is produced quarterly and has a worldwide circulation, is available to members at special rates.

An information booklet produced by the Association contains lists of places such as Museums of special interest to Weavers, book stockists, tuition, small commercial mills and workshops, dyers and finishers, suppliers of dyestuffs, fleeces, equipment, yarns and a list of Guilds. Price is £1.00 in Great Britain.

Summer schools organised by the Association have special rates for affiliated Guild members.

The national exhibition of the Association, staged every other year in different parts of the country, is an opportunity for Guilds to submit their members' works. Slides of all major Association Exhibitions and Schools are available for hire for affiliated Guild meetings.

For further information please contact: Isabella Ricketts, Hon. Secretary, 3 Gillsland Road, Edinburgh, Scotland, EH10 5BW.

The Costume Society

Formed in 1965 to promote the study and preservation of significant examples of historic and contemporary costume. It embraces the documentation of surviving examples and the study of the decorative arts allied to the study of dress, as well as the literary and pictorial sources.

Its Journal, *Costume*, contains articles by experts on the history and technology of costume and covers the whole field of the Society's interests. It is published annually and is supplied free to members.

Membership and general enquiries: Hon. Secretary, Costume Society, Miss Naomi Tarrant, c/o The Royal Scottish Museum, Chambers Street, Edinburgh, Scotland, EH1 1JF.

The Doll Club

An association formed in 1953 to ensure the preservation of old and interesting dolls, dolls' houses and accessories. By organising exhibitions and displays of dolls with lectures, expeditions, competitions and discussion groups, the Club enables members to share and increase their knowledge and to compare collections. The newsletter, *Plangon*, keeps members in touch with each other and the activities of the Club. There are regional branch clubs in various areas.

Write, with stamped addressed envelope to: The Secretary, The Doll Club, Mrs Gillian M. Kernon, Brighton House, 8 The Avenue, Clevedon, Avon, BS21 7GB. (Tel. Clevedon 872241).

Embroiderers' Guild

The Embroiderers' Guild, an educational charity founded in 1906, is open to anyone interested in embroidery.

Its headquarters at Hampton Court Palace are open to members and here the Guild houses a world famous collection of historical embroidery, a library and bookshop and holds classes, workshops and study sessions. For home study or teaching members may borrow folios of embroidery samples, photographs, slides, notes and suggested reading lists as well as books from the extensive library. There are regular exhibitions, social events and outings to places famous for their embroideries. Members receive a twice-yearly Newsletter.

There are over 100 affiliated Branches of the Embroiderers' Guild throughout the U.K. Each Branch arranges its own programme of events and subscription rate. Branch members receive the Newsletters and may borrow books and folios from Headquarters through their Branch Secretary, but have to pay extra to attend events at Headquarters.

The Young Embroiderers' Society, for the under-18 year olds, have their own workshops, classes and Newsletters.

Embroidery, the Guild's quarterly magazine, is available by subscription through the Guild or newsagents.

Further details of all the Guild's activities and facilities from: The Secretary, Embroiderers' Guild, Apt 41A, Hampton Court Palace, East Molesey, Surrey, KT8 9AU. (Tel: 01-943 1229).

The Fan Circle International

Established in 1975 to promote interest and knowledge of the fan in all its aspects – historical, geographical and material conservation. A very active and friendly society with a varied programme of events and meetings. By 1983 four very diverse exhibitions had been held in different parts of the country, mostly in conjunction with a museum and where members were invited to exhibit their own fans, if suitable. Currently, three Bulletins a year are published, giving details of forthcoming lectures and group meetings as well as articles, reports of auction sales, advertisements etc. World-wide membership, with contacts in America, Australia and Europe.

For further information (s.a.e. please) from: The Hon. Sec., Mrs J. Morris, 24 Asmuns Hill, London, NW11 6ET.

The Lace Guild

Formed in 1976 with the object of providing a focus for the promotion of knowledge of lace, its making, study, collecting, history and use and to set standards of teaching and quality of workmanship, to encourage design, to ensure that supplies of necessary materials for the craft remain available, to promote classes, courses and exhibitions, discussions and lectures, to publish a newsletter as a means of communication between all those interested in lace and to raise funds to further the objectives of the Guild, which now has a worldwide membership. The Guild publishes a quarterly magazine, *Lace*.

Further details from: The Hon. Sec., Mrs Jean Buckle, 1 Wychwood, Little Kingshill, Great Missenden, Bucks., HP16 0EU. (s.a.e. please).

NADFAS – The National Association of Decorative and Fine Arts Societies

Founded in 1968 to increase the knowledge and care of the fine arts. A registered charity, with over 150 member societies throughout the country providing monthly illustrated lectures and study groups.

The Voluntary Conservation Corps has NADFAS members actively helping in the preservation of the heritage, undertaking a variety of tasks which include guiding, garden stewarding; cleaning silver, armour or ceramics; indexing; cataloguing; refurbishing a library or helping at one of the Textile Conservation Centres. No work is undertaken without training being given. Study Groups, Seminars and courses are arranged at both national and local level to give the VCC members a greater background knowledge of conservation.

Other divisions of NADFAS include Church Recorders and Young NADFAS.

For further information contact: The Hon. Sec., NADFAS, 38 Ebury Street, London, SW1W OLU.

The Oriental Rug and Textile Society of Great Britain

Started after the first International Conference on Oriental Carpets, which took place in London in 1976 and indicated a renewed interest in the subject. Talks as well as occasional visits to collections, 'show and tells' and films are provided at a modest subscription charge which covers admission to eight events and two newsletters annually. Although both trade and public are welcome as members, there is a firm policy to keep the society independent. Membership has remained constant at about 200, covering a wide range of specialised and general interests which is reflected in the subjects of the talks. It is hoped that this approach encourages students of all ages to contribute to the subject. Meetings are often held in the Polish Hearth Club near the Victoria & Albert Museum, with which the Society continues to have a close informal relationship.

For more information please contact: Miss Lucy Fisher, Administrative Sec., ORTS, 36 Montpelier Road, London, N.W.5.

Quilters' Guild

Membership is open to anyone who either works in patchwork, appliqué or quilting or has specialist interest in quilts. The aims of the Guild are to promote the art of patchwork and quiltmaking and to encourage and maintain high standards of workmanship and design in quiltmaking. Both traditional and contemporary work is equally important within the Guild.

For further details and enquiries contact: The Hon. Sec., Miss Margaret Petit, 56 Wilcot Road, Pewsey, Wilts., SN9 5EL, enclosing a stamped, self-addressed envelope.

The Royal School of Needlework

It is based at 25 Princes Gate, London, SW7 1QE.

The workroom, under the supervision of Miss Margaret Bartlett, B.E.M., undertakes commissions, repairs and cleans lace and samplers. It conserves and restores antique embroideries and tapestries; stretches canvases and makes banners to order. Under an apprenticeship scheme, pupils are taught all forms of highly specialised needlework techniques.

The design room, under the supervision of Miss Cynthia Mitchell, interprets customers' requirements into individual designs.

The Royal School of Needlework Shop is open Monday to Friday, 9.30 a.m. to 5.30 p.m. and stocks all embroidery requirements and books. Personal callers are welcomed and country customers invited to use our fast and efficient mail order service. A price list and colour catalogue of designs are available. (Direct line for orders: 01-584 4893.)

R.S.N. and I.L.E.A. classes: the school has day, evening and short courses in embroidery and lace making for both skilled embroiderers and amateurs. Intensive courses in Easter and Summer holidays (accommodation can be arranged in August) and a correspondence course. Enquiries and bookings: The Class Secretary. (Direct line: 01-584 6179.)

Friends of the Royal School of Needlework subscriptions support the training of apprentices to the workroom. The annual subscription of £8 (£7 covenant) brings a quarterly newsletter, free advice on embroidery one day a month, 10% discount in the shop and reduction on class fees.

A History of the Royal School is available, £2 post free.

The exhibition of antique embroideries in our entrance hall is permanently on display and group visits to the workroom can be arranged by appointment. (S.a.e. with all enquiries is appreciated).

The Textile Conservation Centre

Set up in April 1975 as a registered charitable company with the aims of:

1 providing training in textile conservation to a high standard;

2 offering a service of textile conservation to owners and custodians of public bodies, mu-

seums and other collections and to private individuals;

3 providing advice for the safe-keeping and conservation of historic textiles;

4 researching into all aspects of textile conservation.

Training takes the form of:

1 recognised three-year post-graduate Diploma Courses run with the Courtauld Institute of Art, University of London;

2 in-service apprenticeships in tapestry conservation leading to the Centre's own certificate;

3 internships for sponsored students from other courses or institutions which can be specially arranged.

The Centre receives no regular grant aid and therefore has to rely financially on its earnings from fees for training and conservation commissions, and the generosity of other charitable orgnaisations, including The Friends of the Textile Conservation Centre, who arrange an open day every year on or about 18 May. Other group visits to the Centre can be arranged by prior appointment.

Enquiries of all kinds, including requests for particulars of courses and services offered by the Centre should be addressed to: The Principal, Textile Conservation Centre, Apartment 22, Hampton Court Palace, East Molesey, Surrey, KT8 9AU. (Stamps or two international postal coupons, if applicable, would be appreciated for a reply.)

Societies: U.S.A.

The Costume Society of America publish a newsletter. They can be contacted c/o The Costume Institute, The Metropolitan Museum of Art, Fifth Avenue at 82nd Street, New York, New York 10028, U.S.A.

Inf. No. 4 Oct. 1979

The Textile Conservation Centre Volunteers and conservation

We, in the Textile Conservation Centre, believe that the aims of volunteers in offering their time and services are the same as those of professional conservators, namely to save those objects of the past which are considered important.

However, in regard to textile conservation, it may be necessary to establish a code of practice agreed to by all concerned, or the efforts of volunteers may result in damage rather than conservation because of the extreme vulnerability of old and fragile textiles.

It is essential that volunteers should be willing to accept instructions and carry them out with an unfailing sense of responsibility and integrity.

Organisers of any large-scale voluntary undertaking should recognise that difficulties can arise. Members taking part may have other commitments which could over-ride their voluntary activities. This can make it difficult to command adherence even to apparently agreed arrangements.

Should disagreements occur in any voluntary scheme involving textile conservation the standard of work will, inevitably, be affected. A project which attracts volunteers but which is, nevertheless, labour-intensive, cannot afford to lose its attraction, otherwise the unpaid labour force will not remain until the work is complete.

It would be a pity if the vagaries of fashionable ideas, the pressure of the times in which we live, or the difficulty of maintaining a happy atmosphere over a long period of repetitive work requiring a high standard of achievement, were to be the decisive factors in whether National treasures are to be lost or saved for the future.

It would also be a great loss if the profession of textile conservator failed to attract, train and retain in employment the right type of person because of confusion about what can reasonably be expected from volunteers and what is the province of the fully trained textile conservator.

What then are the areas in which volunteers can be of assistance?

Broadly speaking, we think that volunteers can best be used in preventive conservation, such as in preparing and helping with the organisation of opening a house to the public.

1 by fitting visually acceptable blinds and curtains to fit in with existing surroundings and by seeing that they are used to exclude light whenever possible.

2 by making stylistically suitable loose covers for upholstered furniture so that these can be left on even during visiting hours, except for allowing one chair or sofa to be uncovered, in rotation.

3 by making case covers for the protection of bed hangings and tapestries.

4 by making drugget or baize covers for important carpets.

5 by making sure that special carpets or covers are provided for visitors to walk on so that the grit and dust from their footwear does not damage more precious pieces of floor covering.

6 by cleaning, and keeping clean and free from pests, the surroundings of textile objects – furniture, etc.

7 by preparing important objects for storage either for the period of seasonal closure of the house or to await professional conservation treatment.

8 by giving general maintenance and repair to replacement and supporting textiles such as loose covers, blinds and protective curtains.

9 volunteers who have had instruction in the principles of preventive conservation can assist in the care of the contents of a house by looking for and devising ways to minimise the damage which can be caused by environmental conditions – light, variations of temperature and humidity, static electricity, handling of objects etc. and, with personal contact and knowledge of the conditions of the house, can help to overcome these hazards.

10 by fund-raising.

The Textile Conservation Centre itself is grateful for receiving voluntary help for secretarial work, typing, filing, photography, for cataloguing the library and study collection and for special research when needed.

Experts in various fields are helping with objects belonging to organisations in which they are personally involved and which require repetitive time-consuming conservation treatment, and with the sometimes equally time-consuming documentary aspects of our work.

It is important to preserve the unique aspects of each of the great houses of Britain. Museum collections may, legitimately, be used to achieve the idealised look of fashion plates – whether they are of dress or interior design – but, for a great house to have meaning in the fullest sense as a monument of its past, it should remain as when it was lived in, because it is often only the organic growth of the contents of these houses and their associations with the people who lived there that gives meaning to an individual object and its place in time.

One of the most important and worthwhile areas in which volunteers, especially those with an interest in history, can help, is by doing research and documentation on the objects on view. This is very time-consuming and therefore expensive work, but the results of such research, incorporated in the guide book, would add greatly to the understanding and knowledge which a visit to a great house can give.

Inf. No. 3 Issue 2 March 1982

The Textile Conservation Centre Definitions

Conservation
as a general term may be used to cover a number of different forms of treatment.
The following definitions are those used at the Textile Conservation Centre.

Conservation
is concerned with the safe-keeping of objects as

examples of their kinds and periods.
Conservation treatment must neither add to nor take away from the original but only make it safe for display, storage or future study.

Restoration

aims to make objects look and function according to the intention of their original makers by reproducing worn or missing parts with new materials. Traditional workmanship may or may not be used.

Maintenance or preventive conservation

means to keep and support objects in any particular state so that they do not suffer or their condition does not decline, by providing good conditions (i.e. a clean controlled climate, and protection from light) with constant supervision.

Repair and renovation

may prolong the functioning capacity of an object by removing or altering unwanted parts and substituting worn or missing parts with pieces from another object.

Conservation treatment

is applied to Historic Textiles *on public display*; *in reserve collections* or storage; *in private collections* where they are available for study and research but not otherwise seen by the general public.

Many different fibres, dyes and construction techniques have been involved in producing these textiles and their survival depends largely on the professional training and scientific knowledge possessed by the people responsible for their care and conservation.

Restoration

is applied to objects still in ordinary use and where the design is an integral part of the fabric, as in the dark coloured areas of tapestries and carpets. When the composition of the design has disintegrated along with the oxidised remains of the black or brown weft yarns, the white warp yarns will be exposed with consequent distortion of the design. This may be remedied but other restoration techniques are not normally used at the Textile Conservation Centre because restoration of textiles is costly and – in the long term – rarely successful.

There are several reasons for this lack of success. In the visual sense one reason is that artists and craftsmen of one age do not share the ideals of another age and restoration would inevitably interfere with the designer's original intentions and cause the object to cease to be a statement of its own time.

In the practical sense another reason is that the many variables involved in the production of yarns and dyes and their rates of fading and decay may have the effect of changing apparently successful restoration into damage after a few years.

Maintenance or good housekeeping

practices provide the foundation for the continued existence of any object left to us from the past. Given sound maintenance practices, the time-consuming, and therefore expensive, work of conservation may be postponed and perhaps not become necessary for many years, though it must be considered that the long term survival of any textile object kept in open conditions is problematical.

Repair and renovation

techniques are used to maintain furnishings and curtains of no great age or intrinsic merit, so that they may continue to provide the setting for other objects of historic value.

It is on the quality of the daily maintenance that much of our national – and international – heritage depends, and this is an area where voluntary work by disciplined hands and informed minds may be welcomed and put to good use.

Lack of professionally trained guidance combined with inexperience sometimes results in an inability to evaluate the size and complexity of a project. Consequently damage has been caused, and volunteer groups would be advised to work only under the supervision of trained conservators.

Further reading

A collection of books dealing with textiles is equipment of a different, but still important, kind. Books are part of the necessary tools for almost all activities. Some of the suggested books may be out of print but should still be available through a library. Each book has its own bibliography and further reading can continue and be directed along those lines where the greatest interest lies.

ARNOLD, JANET, *A Handbook of Costume*, Macmillan, London, 1973.
Patterns of Fashion 1660–1860, Wace, London, 1964.
Patterns of Fashion 1860–1940, Macmillan, London, 1966.

BRITISH MUSEUM, *Clothes Moths and Carpet Beetles*, Natural History and Economic Series No. 14, London, 1967.

BURNHAM, DOROTHY, *Warp and Weft*, Royal Ontario Museum, 1980.

CLABBURN, PAMELA, *Needleworkers' Dictionary*, Macmillan, London, 1968.

CLARK, LESLIE L., *The Craftsman in Textiles*, G. Bell & Sons, London, 1968.

COOK, J. GORDON, *Handbook of Textile Fibres*: *Vol. 1 Natural Fibres*; *Vol. 2 Man-made Fibres*, Merrow Publishing Co., Waterford, 4th ed. 1968.

GALE, ELIZABETH, *From Fibres to Fabrics*, Allman & Son, London, 1968.

GOSTELOW, MARY, (consultant ed.) *Complete Guide to Needlework*, Phaidon, London, 1982.

HALD, MARGRETHE, *Ancient Danish Textiles from Bogs and Burials*, National Museum of Denmark, 1980.

HESS, FRED, *Chemistry made simple*, W.H. Allen, London, 1955.

JONES, MARY EIRWEN, *A History of Western Embroidery*, Studio Vista, London, 1969.

LEENE, DR J.E. (ed.), *Textile Conservation*, Butterworths, London, 1972.

LEVY, SANTINA, *Lace, a History*, Maney & Son Ltd, 1983.

MUSEUM ASSOCIATION LEAFLETS, (34 Bloomsbury Way, London, W.C.1), No. 6, *Lighting in Museums*, Gary Thomson and Linda Bullock, 1980; No. 24, *Relative Humidity in Museums*, Gary Thomson and Linda Bullock, 1980.

SEVENSMA, W.S., *Tapestries*, Merlin Press, London, 1965.

SPEISER, NOEMI, *The Manual of Braiding*, pub. by the author, Basle, 1983.

SWAN, JUNE, *Shoes*, (in series 'Costume Accessories', ed. by Dr Aileen Ribeiro), Batsford, London, 1983.

TARRANT, NAOMI, *Collecting Costume*, Allen & Unwin, London, 1983.

THOMSON, GARY, *The Museum Environment*, Butterworth, London, 1978.

Stockists

U.K. & Europe

Bump interlining
MacCulloch & Wallis
25 Dering St
London W.1

F.R. Street Ltd
Textile Merchants
406 St Johns St
London E.C.1

many sewing supply stores

Cardboard boxes (acid free)
Atlantis Paper Co.
Gullivers Wharf
105 Wapping Lane
London E.1

Crepeline

polyester
Schweizerische Seidengazefabric AG
Grutlistrasse 68
Postfach CH 8027
ZÜRICH 2
Switzerland

pure silk
Paul L.G. Dulac et Cie
3 rue Romarin
5 Place du Griffon
Lyons
France

De-ionising equipment
Elga Ltd
Lane End
Buckingham HP14 3JH

Embroidery frames
Royal School of Needlework
25 Princes Gate
London S.W.7
or
specialist needlework shops

Embroidery threads
(e.g. Appleton's crewel wools, Anchor
  stranded embroidery cotton, D.M.C.
  embroidery threads)
Royal School of Needlework (see above)
or
Harrods
Knightsbridge
London S.W.1
or
De Denne
159/161 Kenton Rd
Kenton
Harrow
Middlesex, HA3 OEU
or
Irish Linen Depot
39 Bond St
Ealing
London W.5
or
needlework shops

Filters against ultra violet light

sleeves for tubes and bulbs
The Morden Co.
7 Lytham Rd
Heald Green
Cheadle
Cheshire

varnish (Anti-Sol)
John Chamberlain
88 Wensley Rd
Woodthorpe
Nottingham
or
John Ridley
Alma House
Alma St
Sherwood Rise
Nottingham

Linen

for lining tapestries
F.R. Street (see above)
or
Irish Linen Depot (see above)

thread
Pocock Bros Ltd
235 Southwark Bridge Rd
London
SE1 6NN

Melinex
(sheet plastic coated with a mirror finish)

Transatlantic Plastics
45 Victoria Rd
Surbiton
Surrey

Monofilament Screening
(filtration fabric)

Picreator Enterprises Ltd
44 Park View Gardens
London
NW4 2PN

Needles

sewing – various sizes
Henry Millward & Sons Ltd
Studley
Warwickshire
or
sewing supply stores

curved (surgical)
Surgicraft
Britten St
Redditch
Hereford & Worcestershire

Net

wholesale
Black Bros & Boden
53 Stoney St
Nottingham

retail
Picreator Enterprises (see above)
or
fabric shops

Permutit
(water softening equipment)

Permutit Domestic Division
The Priory
Burnham
Slough
Bucks

Perspex No. 3 Polish
craft shops

Pins

brass, lace, 1 in (2.5 cm) ARTFT 920
MacCulloch & Wallis (see above)
or
lace equipment suppliers

entomological pins size 0

Watkins & Doncaster
Four Throws
Hawkhurst
Kent

glass-headed dressmaker's pins
sewing supply stores

Polythene sheeting
Transatlantic Plastics (see above)

Pulley and ropes for hoists
yachting suppliers

Silica gel crystals
Picreator Enterprises Ltd (see above)

Saponaria (washing agent)
Culpeper House
21 Bruton St
London W.1

Silk fabrics (including crepeline)
Combier Silks Ltd
Langham House
302–308 Regent Street
London W.1

Supporting and lining fabrics
fabric shops

Synperonic NDB (formerly Lissapol)
 washing agent
Frank Joel Ltd
Old Meadow Rd
Hardwick Estate
King's Lynn
Norfolk

Tissue paper (acid free)
L. Gimbert Ltd
Unit 39
Meadow Mills
Water St
Stockport
SK1 2BX
or
Atlantis Paper Co. (see above)
or
Falkiner Fine Papers
117 Long Acre
Covent Garden
London
WC2E 2PA

  small quantities
F.W. Woolworth
or
most stationery suppliers

Untreated cotton lawn and limbric
The Society of Dyers and Colorists

Perkin House
Gratton Road
Bradford
Yorks

Velcro
most haberdashery departments

Washing table
Frank Joel Ltd (see above)

Other conservation equipment
Frank Joel Ltd (see above)

Other conservation materials
Picreator Enterprises Ltd (see above)

General sewing equipment
MacCulloch & Wallis (see above)

U.S.A.

Crepeline pure silk
Exotic Thai Silks
393 Main, Los Altos
California 94022

Embroidery cottons
D.M.C. Corporation
107 Trumbull St
Elizabeth
New Jersey 07206

Embroidery frames
The Stitchery
204 Worcester St
Wellesley Hills
Massachusetts 02181

General sewing materials
Abe Bloom & Sons Inc.
137 West 23rd St
New York
NY 10011

Index

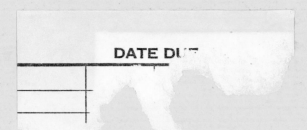

DATE DUE